Clementine Churchill

First published in 2015 as *First Lady: The Life and Wars of Clementine Churchill* by
Aurum Press Ltd, an imprint of the Quarto Group. This abridged edition first published
in 2019 by White Lion Publishing, an imprint of The Quarto Group.
The Old Brewery, 6 Blundell Street
London N7 9BH
United Kingdom

T (0)20 7700 6700

www.QuartoKnows.com

A catalogue record for this book is available from the British Library.

ISBN 978 1 78131 909 3

Ebook ISBN 978 1 78131 910 9

10 9 8 7 6 5 4 3 2 1

Publisher Jessica Axe
Commissioning Editor Melissa Hookway
Editorial Director Jennifer Barr
Designer Isabel Eeles
Abridger Steve Gove
Copy Editor Aruna Vasudevan
Production Controller Robin Boothroyd
Project Editor Emma Bastow
Picture Research Angelika Pirkl

Printed in China

SONIA PURNELL

Clementine Churchill

A Life in Pictures

WHITE LION
PUBLISHING

For Jon, Laurie and Joe

·

With all my love

'I send this token, but how little
can it express my gratitude to you for
making my life & any work I have done
possible, and for giving me so much
happiness in a world of accident & storm.'

Winston to Clementine, on their fortieth wedding
anniversary, 12 September 1948, Cap d'Antibes

CONTENTS

FOREWORD

I was already midway into playing 'Clemmie' in the television series *The Crown* when this wonderful biography came out and it was like a whirlwind of fresh air to me, a door being opened from a tiny crack into a flood of sunlight. I had already soaked up everything that Mary Soames had written about her mother and the letters between her parents, and I had tried to get behind the eyes in the public face that looked out at me from Clemmie's photos. I was brimful of her but I knew I would have to hold back so much. In *The Crown*, as in life, Clemmie would be seen as a supporting role.

Sonia Purnell gets behind the supporting role and puts Clementine Churchill at the heart of the story. Most male-centred history books are only interested in women for the light they may throw on the Great Man, as the power behind the throne. For me, Clementine was not so much 'behind' Churchill as alongside him, supplying fortitude when his own failed, sensitivity when he lacked it, often disagreeing with him privately but always supporting him publicly. Sonia Purnell confirmed me in that view and has placed in the public domain everything I was struggling to communicate in a small corner of the small screen.

One thing I did manage to influence as a result of reading *First Lady,* was the filming of the destruction of Graham Sutherland's portrait of Churchill. Clemmie wanted rid of the object that caused her husband so much distress, and in the original script she silently looked on as a removal man smashed the painting to smithereens with a mallet. Luckily, we hadn't shot the scene yet and when I found out the true story in this book (see page 205) I passed it on to the team and, thanks to their responsiveness, the scene was re-written and became one of the most memorable visual sequences in the whole series. I shan't spoil it here. I will just say that flames supplanted the mallet. I am proud to have been a link in that chain of information.

What struck me above all about the incident was that Clemmie had told her private secretary that 'no one need know' what had happened. She said this mainly to protect her staff from blame, but for me it also pinpointed the habit of mind of that generation and class. It is a combination of 'what we do is no one else's business' and the wartime expediency of information being restricted on a 'need to know' basis.

But it also exemplifies the tantalising reticence of women in general and in particular of Clementine Churchill, who never wanted to be publicly known. Don't worry, Clemmie, we realise that no one book or performance can ever sum up a life, but we hope you understand that with so many millions of words written by and about your husband, we have a great need to know more about you.

Harriet Walter

INTRODUCTION

Late on the evening of Monday 5 June 1944, Clementine Churchill walked past the Royal Marine guards into the Downing Street Map Room. Wearing an elegant silken housecoat that covered her nightdress, her beautiful face still fully made up, she looked immaculate and, as always, serene. Around her, though, the atmosphere in the heart of British military command was palpably tense, even frayed. She glanced at the team of grave-faced 'plotters' busily tracking troops, trucks and ships on their charts. Then she cast her eyes over the long central table, from which the phones never stopped ringing, to the far corner where, as she expected, she spotted Winston, shoulders hunched, jowly face cast in agonised brooding. She went to him as she knew she must, for no one else, no aide, no general, no friend however loyal, could help him now.

Clementine was one of a tiny group privy to the months and years of top-secret preparations for the next morning's monumental endeavour. Fully apprised of the risks of what would be the largest seaborne invasion in history, she knew, too, the unthinkable price of failure: millions of people and a vast swathe of Europe would remain under Nazi tyranny, their hopes of salvation dashed. Uniquely, however, she also understood the ghosts that haunted Winston that night, thinking as he was of the thousands of men he had sent to their deaths in the Dardanelles campaign of the First World War. She alone had sustained him both through that disaster and the horrors of his time serving in the trenches on the Western Front. Now, tens of thousands more were to risk their lives in northern France. Huge convoys were already moving through the darkness towards their battle stations off the coast of Normandy. He had delayed the D-Day operation for as long as he could to ensure the greatest chance of success, but now British, American and Canadian troops would, in a few hours, attempt to take a heavily fortified coastline defended by what were regarded as the world's best soldiers.

Earlier that evening, Winston and Clementine had discussed the prospects of the gambit's success again, at length and alone over a candlelit dinner. No doubt he had poured out his fears and she had sought, as so many times before, to stiffen his resolve. Yet it could be put off no longer; the command to proceed had been given. Raising his face as she approached, Winston turned to his wife and asked, rhetorically: 'Do you realise that by the time you wake up in the morning, twenty thousand men may have been killed?'[1]

To the outside world Winston Churchill showed neither doubt nor weakness. Since he had declared to the world in June 1940 that Britain would 'never surrender', his had become the voice of defiance, strength and valour. Even Stalin, one of Winston's fiercest critics, was to concede that he could think of no other instance in history when the future of the world had so depended on the courage of a single man.[2] But what enabled this extraordinary figure to stand up to Hitler when others all around him were crumbling? How did he find in himself the strength to command men to go to their certain deaths? How could an ailing heavy drinker and cigar-smoker well into his sixties carry such a burden for five long years while cementing an unlikely coalition of allies that not only saved Britain, but ultimately defeated the Axis?

Winston's conviction, his doctor Lord Moran observed while tending him through the war, began 'in his own bedroom'. This national saviour and global legend was in some ways a man like any other; he was not an emotional island devoid of the need for personal sustenance, as so many historians have depicted him. His resolve drew on someone else's. In fact, Winston's upbringing and temperament made him almost vampiric in his hunger for the love and energy of others. Violet Asquith, who adored him all her life, noted that he was 'armed to the teeth for life's encounter' but 'also strangely vulnerable' and in want of 'protection'.[3]

Only one person was able and willing to provide that 'protection' whatever the challenge, as she showed on that critical June night in 1944. Yet Clementine's role as Winston's wife, closest adviser and greatest influence was overlooked for much of her life, and has been largely forgotten in the decades since.

Neither mousy nor subservient, as many assume her to have been, Clementine was so much more than a mere extension of her husband's career

Clementine suffered from chronic nervous ill health in the mid-1930s and often travelled overseas to avoid tensions at home. Here she is in Salzburg, Austria, in 1935 in the company of William Somerset Maugham

and ego. Like him, she relentlessly privileged the national interest above her own health, safety and family; her list of extra-marital achievements would put many present-day government ministers, speech-writers, charity chiefs, ambassadors, activists, spin doctors, MPs and hospital managers to shame. Unlike Winston, though, she was capable of great empathy, and had a surer grasp of the importance of public image. In her trend-setting sense of style she was a precursor to Jackie Onassis – being known particularly for her leopard-skin coats and colourful chiffon turbans – and as a hostess she was renowned across the globe for her elegant hospitality; her skills at the diplomatic dinner table won the admiration of Charles de Gaulle, and played a crucial role in binding America to Britain's cause. For all this and more, she was honoured by three British monarchs, and also by the Soviet Union. But just surviving, let alone shaping, what must surely count as one of the twentieth century's most challenging marriages would have been a notable triumph in itself.

Winston once claimed that, after their wedding they, had simply 'lived happily ever after'. That is stretching the truth – never was there a break from the 'whirl of haste, excitement and perpetual crisis'[4] that surrounded them. She could not even go to talk to him in the bathroom without on occasion finding members of the Cabinet in there, too, half-hidden by the steam. Nor were their exchanges always gentle. They rowed frequently, often epically, and it was not for nothing that he sometimes referred to her as 'She-whose-commands-must-be-obeyed'.[5] An opinionated figure in her own right, she was unafraid to reprimand him for his 'odious' behaviour,[6] or to oppose privately his more noxious political beliefs; gradually she altered his Victorian outlook with what he called her 'pinko' ideas, and even her support for women's rights. But however furiously they might disagree, she loved him for his undoubted compassion, and revelled in her union with a man so 'exciting' and 'famous'. For his part, he simply doted and depended on her.

Throughout the first three decades of their marriage, Winston and Clementine were united by a common project: making him Prime Minister. When that day arrived their aim changed, becoming survival itself. And in peacetime, whatever her misgivings about his refusal to give up politics, they were jointly dedicated to his legacy. Not only did they weather repeated public and personal humiliation together, they overcame the bitterest of personal tragedies, and survived the all but intolerable strains of being at the centre of two world wars. In so doing they forged one of the most important partnerships in history. The question is not simply what did she do for him, but also what could he have done without her?

Even so, this formidable woman has virtually no public presence in popular history. While he is understandably one of the most analysed figures of all time, the preternaturally private Clementine has remained overlooked and unexplained. She is so elusive that there are differing views on such basic questions as the colour of her eyes (grey, blue or hazel-brown?[7]) and hair (ash-blonde, brown or red?[8]). Many people think Winston's wife was the 'American one', when in fact it was his mother Jennie who hailed from the US. Consult certain biographies of her husband and Clementine features as barely more than a passing acquaintance. The index of Nigel Knight's *Churchill: The Greatest Briton Unmasked*, for instance, contains not a single reference to her. Others, such as Richard Hough, author of *Winston & Clementine: The Triumph & Tragedies of the Churchills*, go so far as to claim that she was a 'nuisance' who added to, rather than reduced, the pressures on her husband.

It is certainly true that Clementine was sometimes rigid and unforgiving, but in these traditionally minded, one-sided accounts Winston's own testament to what she meant to him and his life's work has been conveniently underplayed or misconstrued. So have the perspectives of the many generals, politicians, civil servants and diplomats who worked closely with them both and became her fervent admirers. Even Lord Beaverbrook, the buccaneering newspaper magnate who was for a long time her most loathed personal enemy, became in the end a devoted fan. It is ironic and telling that many of these observers are far better known than she.

Today we are fascinated by the deeds and dress of our contemporary First Ladies, on both sides of the Atlantic. In a different era Clementine largely, if not wholly, escaped such media scrutiny and hardly courted the press on her own account – even though she was a skilful operator on behalf of her chosen causes. Yet she was more powerful and in some ways more progressive than most, if not all, of her modern successors. Moreover, many of the struggles she endured still resonate – not least the gruelling inner turmoil Winston found it so difficult to understand, or help her with. It is high time for a fresh appraisal of the woman behind his greatness, one that may allow her contribution to be duly recognised.

The only major previous account of Clementine's life – an admirable book by the Churchills' daughter, Mary Soames – was, although later revised, first published nearly forty years ago. In any case, it understandably treats its subject almost exclusively from the family's viewpoint, with conspicuous gaps in the story. Since then many revealing papers – such as the Pamela Harriman collections at the Library of Congress in Washington DC – have been released, or have come to light for the first time, and several former staff have opened up about their experiences. What fascinates over and over again is the strength of the impression Clementine made on so many third parties, including allies from Russia, Canada, Australia and America, as well as those who witnessed her in action closer to home. Some contemporaries recorded a 'physical shock' on meeting her for the first time. Who would have guessed that she laughed louder than Winston? That she was taller than him and decidedly more athletic? That he cried more than her and owned more hats? That the camera never quite captured her startling beauty and that she could, like a princess, lift a room merely by entering it? Or that she was not the paradigm of an upper-class matron but the surprising product of a broken home, a suburban grammar school, a lascivious mother and a formative year spent in and around the fish market at Dieppe?

This is not a history of either world war, nor another study of Winston Churchill from an alternative vantage point, though oft neglected aspects of his character do come to the fore. It is instead a portrait of a shy girl from a racy background who was related to Britain's most glamorous aristocratic family (in more ways than one), but was looked down upon by her mother,

Clementine receives an enthusiastic welcome from workers in the Tyneside docks and shipyards during a tour in 1947. She learned how to work a crowd during her many decades in the public eye.

and disdained by the dominant political dynasty of her day. It is the story of someone who feared casinos and bailiffs, and struggled to bond with her children. It is an attempt to recover the memory of a woman who married the man variously described as 'the largest human being of our times' and 'the stuff of which tyrants are made'. (That he never became one is in no small part down to her.) Even before 1940, Clementine's life was packed with drama, heartache and endurance. But, colourful and troubled as it was, this was merely a lengthy and exhaustive apprenticeship for her critical role as First Lady during her country's 'death fight' for survival.

Prior to Clementine, Britain had known merely the 'politician's wife', opinionated perhaps, but rarely directly involved in government business. Today, we have much the same; women glossed up for the cameras on set-piece occasions, thin, smiling and silent. Her immediate successors – Violet Attlee in 1945 and Clarissa Eden in 1955 – were of markedly lesser ambition and failed to pick up her baton. Clarissa, Anthony Eden's wife, was glamorous, younger, more intellectual and arguably more modern than Clementine (her aunt by marriage), but she lacked a populist touch and admits she was never even briefed on government business, lacking 'the gumption to ask…I can't believe how passive and hopeless I was.'[9] Clementine's post-war successor Mrs Attlee was 'jealous' of the time taken up by her husband's job,[10] and Harold Wilson's wife, Mary, was at first so overawed at being the Prime Minister's spouse that she would be physically sick every morning.[11] Cherie Blair, probably the prime ministerial consort most involved in her husband's role since Clementine, explains the universal predicament: 'There is no job description for the Prime Minister's spouse because there is no job. But there is a unique position that provides for each holder an opportunity and a challenge.'[12] How interesting that a woman born into the Victorian age, who never went to university, had five children and could not vote until in her thirties, should have grasped that opportunity and that challenge with greater ambition and success than those who have come since.

The case can be made that no other premier's wife, in a democratic country at least, has played such a pivotal role in her husband's government – arguably greater during the Second World War than the greatest of American First Ladies, Clementine's direct contemporary, Eleanor Roosevelt. This appears all the more remarkable in light of how poorly defined and resourced the position is at 10 Downing Street in comparison with the White House. From the very earliest days of the Union, the wife of the US President has enjoyed a status that, albeit not enshrined in the constitution itself, provides an official platform for public work and influence, backed by the heavily staffed Office of the First Lady. Clementine had no official staff, role model or guidebook. She in effect invented her wartime role from scratch, and eventually persuaded an initially reluctant government machine to help her.

Yet she never sought glory for her achievements, and rarely received it. She was genuinely astonished when noticed at all. Curiously, it was often visiting Americans who were most observant of the scale of her contribution during the war. The US ambassador Gil Winant was intensely moved when he accompanied her on a tour of bombed-out streets during the Blitz. As she talked to people left with little more of their lives than piles of rubble, he noticed the particularly 'great appreciation' she stirred in middle-aged women, who seemed inspired and uplifted by her presence. Marvelling at the 'deep' and 'significant' looks of empathy that 'flashed between her and these mothers of England' he was puzzled as to why the newspapers or indeed the British government made so little of what she did.[13] Clementine's huge mailbag at the time was full of letters from people grateful for her help; people who viewed her as their champion. But while others, such as the then Queen, have been loudly and widely hailed for their war work, her part in the story seems to have been lost.

'If the future breeds historians of understanding,' Winant wrote shortly after the return of peace, Clementine's 'service to Great Britain' will finally be 'given the full measure [it] deserves'. This book attempts to do just that.

The Churchills at home at Hyde Park Gate on the occasion of Winston's 85th birthday. By now his failing health required the attention of a male nurse as well as Clementine's ever-solicitous eye.

The Level of Events

1885–1908

Fear defined Clementine Hozier's earliest memory. After being deposited by her nurse at the foot of her parents' bed, she saw her mother, Lady Blanche, stretching out her arms towards her. Yet Clementine was frozen to the spot by the sight of her father, Henry, slumbering at her mother's side. 'I was frightened of him,' she explained much later[1]. But by then the damage was done. For all the fortitude Clementine would show in adulthood, the insecurity that had endured from her infancy never left her.

Clementine cut a dash even when sitting in a garden, including wearing her beloved pristine white gloves.

Clementine's mother was the eldest daughter of the tenth Earl of Airlie, whose ancient Scots lineage was enlivened by castle burnings and Jacobite uprisings. Lady Blanche's own mother was a Stanley of Alderley Park in Cheshire, a tribe of assertive and erudite English matriarchs who combined radical Liberal views with upper-class condescension. Champions of female education, the Stanley women had co-founded Girton College in Cambridge in 1869. In contrast, Henry's family had made their money in brewing, gaining entrance to society through the profits of industry rather than the privilege of birth. Lady Blanche's father considered Henry Montague Hozier a 'bounder', while she was herself soon to discover that, after a career giving orders in the Army, he now expected the same unquestioning obedience at home.

Five years after her wedding day, on 15 April 1883, Lady Blanche gave birth to her first child, Kitty. Clementine (rhyming with *mean*) was born two years later, on April Fools' Day. The twins – Nellie and William (Bill) – arrived in 1888. Of the four children, it is now thought likely that none were Hozier's and that there was probably more than one biological father. The first Lord Redesdale, Bertie Mitford (grandfather to the famous Mitford sisters, also incidentally Clementine's second cousins), was considered the most likely sire from Lady Blanche's many lovers. But there were at least two other contenders. London's more respectable drawing rooms were scandalised by such public uncertainty over the children's parentage, with the result that Lady Blanche was regularly snubbed. While she continued to indulge in a life of frantic sexual intrigue, her children were cared for by a succession of grumpy maids and governesses.

In autumn 1891, Hozier sued for divorce and the two elder girls became hostages in a bitter battle over custody and financial support. Clementine was just six when she and Kitty were wrested from their mother to live with Henry and his sister, the spinster Aunt Mary, who believed children benefitted greatly from being whipped. Hozier soon found the girls an inconvenience, quickly packaging them off to a governess, and then to a 'horrible, severe' boarding school in Edinburgh.[2]

•

Clementine was just six when she and Kitty were wrested from their mother to live with Henry and his sister, the spinster Aunt Mary, who believed children benefitted greatly from being whipped.

•

The young timorous Clementine had few friends and was devoted to her dog, Carlo. She never got over his death under the wheels of a train.

Above: Clementine and her elder sister, Kitty, were devoted to each other, but their father, Sir Henry, seen here with them at the family home in Scotland in 1888, was a forbidding figure who inspired fear.

Opposite inset: Lady Blanche, here shown at the age of eight, was a forceful character from her earliest years. Her parents later became eager to marry her off.

Eventually, he allowed Lady Blanche to extract her unhappy daughters and reunite them with their four-year-old twin siblings, Bill and Nellie. Over the following eight years, Lady Blanche and her brood led a peripatetic existence, moving to one set of furnished lodgings after another. In an effort to earn her keep, she wrote culinary articles for the newspapers, but she sometimes found herself too bored or distracted to put food on the table. If her children were sometimes in want of sustenance and maternal attention, they rarely went short of learning, however. Their mother employed full-time Francophone or German governesses and other teachers were brought in as required.

In about 1898, when Clementine was thirteen, Lady Blanche decamped from London for Seaford in Sussex, east of the Channel port of Newhaven. By now Clementine and Kitty were quite different: the former plain and awkward; the latter pretty and flirty, albeit impudent and ruthless. Kitty was her mother's blatant and persistent favourite, but the timid Clementine never showed any jealousy towards her. Each sister found comfort in the other in a somewhat bewildering world.

Lady Blanche, 1852-1925, rarely showed maternal feelings to her shy and withdrawn daughter, Clementine, much preferring her puckish and impudent first-born, Kitty. In any case, Lady Blanche had little time for domestic concerns as she pursued a life of frantic sexual intrigue, reputedly keeping up to ten lovers at a time.

Of the four children, it is now thought likely that none were Hozier's and that there was probably more than one biological father

By the summer of 1899, Hozier had defaulted on the meagre allowance which he had agreed on following the divorce; Lady Blanche was deeply in debt. In July, seemingly out of the blue, the children were told they were moving to France, their mother having long suspected that Hozier might try to snatch back Kitty and Clementine. Although already an adept Francophone, it took Clementine time to adjust to her new life in Dieppe, not least because she constantly felt an outsider among her French peers and struggled to make friends. Yet she led an outdoor life which resulted in her starting to emerge as the striking young woman she was to become.

Lady Blanche relished Dieppe's bohemian ambiance, which attracted foreign writers and artists such as Oscar Wilde, Max Beerbohm and Walter Sickert (who was to become her lover). She also enjoyed the casino. She lost money she did not have and, to Clementine's shame, was reduced to wearing cheap gingham dresses and having to ask for credit in the local shops. Almost as galling were the public rows that her mother engaged in with Madame Villain, Sickert's other mistress and the queen of the Dieppe fish market. Clementine was learning all too young to deal with public humiliation, and her fear of gambling, due to her mother's fascination with it, would never leave her.

One winter's night late in 1899, Lady Blanche's anxiety about her ex-husband's intentions regarding the girls were confirmed. Having tracked them down to Dieppe, Hozier sent invitations to each girl to dine with him individually. Kitty's dinner passed without incident; however, when it came to Clementine's turn, Hozier delivered the dreaded news that she was to come to live with him – or rather with Aunt Mary. Faced with this unthinkable prospect, Clementine's shyness disappeared. With previously undetected determination and courage, she announced calmly that her mother would refuse to allow her to leave Dieppe, made a dash for the door, resisting Hozier's attempts to bar her way, and ran full pelt for home. The captain of the Dieppe–Newhaven steamer later confirmed to Lady Blanche Hozier's intention to kidnap Clementine and take her back to England that same afternoon.

Scarcely had one crisis passed, however, when another came to test Clementine. A few weeks later, in February 1900, her sister, Kitty, contracted typhoid. Clementine and Nellie were sent away to relatives in Scotland. Fearing the effect on Kitty if she knew her sisters were leaving, Lady Blanche told them to say 'goodnight' rather than 'goodbye'. The last the girls saw of

VANITY FAIR   June 10 1904

"The Nobleman of the Garden"

Clockwise from top left: Sir Henry Montague Hozier, appearing here in *Vanity Fair* in February 1883, suffered from an 'absence of humour' and was a 'born autocrat', according to an investigation into his business practices by his employers at Lloyd's of London. He was not interested in having children and is unlikely to have been the biological father of any of Lady Blanche's children.

Bertie — or Algernon Bertram Freeman-Mitford, the 1st Baron Redesdale — is one likely contender to be Clementine's real father. He was also grandfather to the famous Mitford sisters.

Capt. William George Middleton, known as Bay, was another handsome, if in his case melancholic, admirer of Lady Blanche. Later in life he broke his neck steeple-chasing, but he is the second most likely contender to be Clementine's real father.

Nellie Hozier was Clementine's younger sister and the two remained close into their adult years. Clementine and Winston helped her financially when she and her husband, Bertram Romilly, fell on hard times.

Kitty, as they closed the door, was as a silent and emaciated figure confined to bed. Despite all her mother's efforts, Kitty died a month before her seventeenth birthday.

Less than a year after leaving England, the family was uprooted yet again, back to suburban Berkhamsted in Hertfordshire. Despite the tragedy of losing Kitty, Clementine liked her latest home. She was about to embark on what were probably the happiest and certainly the most settled years of her early life. Her time at the local grammar school, Berkhamsted High School for Girls, was to change her outlook completely.

In this steady and studious atmosphere, Clementine thrived. She was promoted to a higher year group for French, and prizes came quickly. In 1901, she won a silver medal for French presented by the French ambassador. Lady Blanche, at last recognising her daughter's potential, treated her to a trip to Paris, along with a former governess. Encouraged by her headmistress, Clementine was secretly nursing dreams of academia, even if university for women was still a comparative novelty. She was further spurred on in her studies by her great-aunt, Maude Stanley, the blue-stocking sister of her maternal grandmother; Maude also introduced her to the exciting world of politics.

In the tussle over Clementine's future, however, Lady Blanche held the trump card. To stop this university nonsense once and for all she approached another relative, the wealthy Lady St Helier, and enlisted her help in launching Clementine into the world to which Lady Blanche deemed she properly belonged. Lady St Helier invited Clementine to stay with her at her distinguished London mansion in Portland Place, near Regent's Park. She took her to lavish balls and glittering dinners, where Clementine was fêted for her beauty. Sure enough, her head was turned. By the time Clementine passed her Higher School Certificate, in the summer of 1903, there was no more talk of academia; the grammar school girl was feeling ever more at home in grand society.

Soon she began to gain suitors, chief among them Sidney Cornwallis Peel, the eligible younger son of a viscount (and grandson of former Prime Minister Sir Robert). He took her to the theatre and sent her white violets every day and proposed. Lady St Helier thought her job was done. But Clementine was a romantic: realising that she was not in love with Sidney, she broke off their engagement, although they later became secretly betrothed. In April 1906, she found her nerve again and parted from him for good.

•

Encouraged by her headmistress, Clementine was secretly nursing dreams of academia, even if university for women was still a comparative novelty.

•

29

Afterwards she seems to have panicked: she needed to escape from her mercurial mother who thought nothing of reprimanding her by boxing her ears. A later engagement to Lionel Earle, a wealthy civil servant with intellectual tastes, was also terminated when, on a fortnight's holiday in the Netherlands, she saw him for the pompous bore he really was.

Now that Nellie had also finished school, Lady Blanche moved to London to take a firmer hand in her daughters' social careers. Clementine had no choice but to earn her keep, supplementing her small allowance by giving French lessons. A year later, she began working for her cousin, Lena Whyte, in her dressmaking business. Needlework bored her, but she learned to make clothes and even hats, for herself as well as for clients. Clementine had inherited her mother's genius for making the simplest outfits elegant, although she was all too aware of the inadequacies of her wardrobe compared to the lavish gowns of her society peers. Nevertheless, she had an advantage – contemporary accounts pour praise on her stunning good looks.

A year after finishing school, during the summer season of 1904, Clementine attended a ball given by Lord and Lady Crewe. Among the guests in this Liberal household was a rising young politician named Winston Churchill. A controversial figure, he was barred from most Conservative homes having defected from the party earlier in the year to join the Liberals. Considered a renegade and class traitor by the Tories, he was viewed as pushy and puffed up, even by admirers. His notorious adventures during the Second Boer War, including a daring escape from a prisoner of war camp, lent him an air of raffish danger. A prolific author as well as a soldier and MP, Winston was already a celebrity.

Upon arriving at the ball, accompanied by his American mother, Jennie, Winston was arrested by the sight of a fawn-like girl alone in a doorway. He stood motionless, staring at her. When Lady Randolph Churchill presented her son to Clementine, the great wordsmith was struck dumb, not even managing the customary invitation to dance. Clementine assumed she had been introduced out of pity, and in any case did not care for what she had heard about this notorious publicity seeker. It was an encounter that left no lasting impression on either of them.

Four years later, Winston, now in his mid-thirties, was being a labelled by the press a confirmed bachelor. One evening in March 1908, Clementine returned home after work to find a message from Lady St Helier, asking her to make up the numbers at a dinner the same evening. The guests were

Above: Clementine Hozier's engagement to Winston Churchill, the rising young politician, was the celebrity news of its day. She was trailed by newspaper photographers even when going for a fitting for her wedding dress and intitially found the attention unsettling.

already starting on the chicken course by the time Winston arrived; he was attending with some reluctance. The wealthy American Ruth Lee wrote in her diary that, having taken a vacant place to the hostess's left, Winston proceeded to ignore her. Instead he 'became suddenly and entirely absorbed in Miss Clementine Hozier and paid her such marked and exclusive attention the whole evening that everyone was talking about it'.[3] Winston's fascination was piqued by one of the very necessities that, in Clementine's eyes, made her an outsider: never before had he met a fashionable young woman at a society dinner who earned her own living. She was, in addition, ethereally lovely – and, influenced by her aunts and her own schooling, she was gripped by the cut and thrust of politics. For Clementine, Winston's gauche behaviour at the ball, four years before, seemed to have given way to a maturity and worldliness that thrilled her.

Thereafter, he wasted little time. Within a couple of weeks, Winston had invited Clementine and Lady Blanche to Salisbury Hall, his mother's house near St Albans, Hertfordshire. In Winston's first letter to Clementine, on 16 April, he wrote about how much he enjoyed their discussions: 'What a comfort & pleasure it was to me to meet a girl with so much intellectual quality & such strong reserves of noble sentiment.'[4]

At that time, it was customary for members of Parliament elevated to the Cabinet to stand for re-election. So while Clementine was on a trip to Germany, the newly promoted Winston began campaigning in his largely working-class seat in north-west Manchester. In one letter to her, he referred in glowing terms to the help given to him by the famously alluring Lady Dorothy Howard, perhaps hoping to prompt a reaction from Clementine. On 23 April, she duly replied: 'I feel so envious of Dorothy Howard – It must be very exciting to feel one has the power of influencing people … I feel as much excited as if I were a candidate.'[5]

This expression of political interest – with its hint of jealous concern – must have greatly pleased Winston. On 27 April, he wrote: 'How I should have liked you to have been there. You would have enjoyed it I think.' He exhibited, moreover, a new mood of measured self-revelation, saying: 'Write to me again. I am a solitary creature in the midst of crowds. Be kind to me.'

Here at last the rumbustious adventurer of popular folklore felt safe enough to admit that he was lonely. For Clementine, who had since Kitty's death felt no one needed her, this was a clear signal that she might have found a new role to play. After Winston lost the Manchester election on

•

Winston's fascination was piqued by one of the very necessities that, in Clementine's eyes, made her an outsider: never before had he met a fashionable young woman at a society dinner who earned her own living.

•

On their engagement Winston wrote to Clementine that there were 'no words to convey to you the feelings of love & joy by which my being is possessed'. Although she also loved him with a passion she felt nervous about exactly what and who she was taking on.

Zur Vermählung des englischen Handelsministers.

Mrs. Winston Churchill, geb. Miß Clementine Hozier. Oben: Mr. Winston Churchill.

23 April, Clementine could not help but admire the way he picked himself up from defeat to win another election in Dundee in the following month. Unusually self-sufficient, she did not tell even close friends about her growing feelings for him, but she was convinced that she was in love.

Clementine saw Winston again several times in June and July of that year, but never alone. Some weeks later, she received an invitation from Winston's cousin, Sunny, the Duke of Marlborough, to visit Blenheim Palace. She was reluctant, but Winston insisted, promising that his mother and Sunny would look after her. After some hesitation, on 10 August, Clementine left the Isle of Wight, where she had been staying, and took the train to Oxfordshire. Walking up the front steps of the grand family seat into the gloom of its great hall, she found Winston, his mother, Jennie, the Duke, Winston's great friend F.E. Smith and his wife, Margaret, plus a private secretary from the Board of Trade, all waiting to greet her. It was clear this was to be no low-key visit.

Over dinner, Winston promised to show Clementine the following morning the famous rose gardens overlooking the lake. Punctual as ever, she descended to breakfast at the appointed hour only to be left waiting. Fearing that she would flounce out, Sunny hastily invited her for a drive around the estate, while sending word up to Winston, who was still in bed. The walk was hastily rearranged for the afternoon.

Winston escorted Clementine on a long tour of the gardens, but nothing of much import had been said by the time they began to make their way back up to the house. Finally, a summer shower drove the couple to take shelter in a little Greek temple folly. Clementine spotted a spider scuttling across the floor, and quietly decided that if Winston had not declared himself before it reached a crack in the flagstones she would leave.[6] Happily, just in time, Winston asked if she would marry him. Without any further unnecessary hesitation, she agreed.

The next day, Clementine left Blenheim with a letter from Winston asking for Lady Blanche's permission to marry her daughter. He could not bear to wait for the answer, though, and at the last moment jumped on the London-bound train beside her.

Lady Blanche considered Winston just right for her unusual offspring. He did not have the fortune or title she would have liked, but he was brilliant and ambitious and could earn his own living – and at least he was marrying for romance rather than money. Having received Lady Blanche's approval, Winston would not brook a long engagement. A date was fixed for the wedding in a month's time.

Opposite: An engagement photograph of the young Miss Clementine Hozier in 1908, with an inset picture of her famous fiancé. Admirers said she had the profile of a queen.

More Than Meets the Eye

1908–14

Clementine later admitted finding her reception as Winston's new fiancée 'petrifying'.[1] Waking up at dawn on her wedding day, 12 September 1908, in a large chilly room in Lady St Helier's mansion did nothing to boost her spirits. She had been exiled from her own home to make room for guests and felt cut off in Portland Place from the bustle of family life. Longing to return for one last taste of the familiar, she crept down the staircase in her dressing gown while the house was still dark and Lady St Helier asleep. Minutes later, a figure slipped out of a back door and hopped on a bus west to Kensington in an outfit borrowed from a kindly young maid.

Clementine and Winston were married on 12 September 1908 at St Margaret's Church, Westminster. Her dress of shimmering white satin and coronet of fresh orange blossom was widely admired. Winston's attire received less favourable reviews, with one magazine unkindly suggesting it gave him the air of a 'glorified coachman'.

DAILY GRAPHIC
ONE PENNY

No. 5852.—Vol. LXXV.

LONDON: MONDAY, SEPTEMBER 14, 1908.

Registered as a Newspaper.

THE MARRIAGE OF A CABINET MINISTER.

THE BRIDESMAIDS.

MR. CHURCHILL AND HIS BRIDE PASSING DOWN THE NAVE AFTER THE MARRIAGE CEREMONY.

THE BRIDEGROOM ARRIVES AT THE CHURCH.
("Daily Graphic" Photograph.)

THE CHURCHILL-HOZIER WEDDING AT ST. MARGARET'S, WESTMINSTER, ON SATURDAY AFTERNOON.   (See page 3.)

1025

She arrived at Abingdon Villas to astonished gasps. A merry time with Nellie and Bill restored her resolve and she soon headed back (by horse-drawn brougham this time) to prepare for the service at St Margaret's in Parliament Square.

Four minutes after the bell of Big Ben struck two o'clock, Clementine entered the church on the arm of her brother, Bill. Draped in shimmering white satin, a veil of tulle clipped to her hair by a coronet of fresh orange blossom, Clementine wore diamond earrings, a gift from Winston, and clutched a bouquet of fragrant white tuberoses and a white parchment prayer book. When it came time to take their vows, Winston's were loud and clear, hers so soft as to be barely audible.

The married couple finally emerged from the church to find cheering crowds thronging the route to the reception back at Portland Place. They spent their first evening as husband and wife at Blenheim, the palace having been tactfully vacated by the Duke. It can only be guessed as to which of the couple was the more nervous. Both were almost certainly virgins and, at nearly thirty-four, Winston's manly pride was at stake. By the time they left Blenheim, a couple of days later, for Italy's Lake Maggiore, it appears the young couple had got the hang of things: within a month of returning from the honeymoon, Clementine was pregnant.

In many ways they were a well-matched couple – two insecure people with much in common. Both had suffered from the lack of a steady, loving childhood and neither formed close friendships easily. Given her own background and her mother's preference for her sister, Clementine could empathise with Winston's pain at his father's disappointment in him and preference for Jack, his younger, less troublesome brother. As children both Winston and Clementine had relied on middle-aged women outside the family for emotional sustenance. Clementine had received the tender

Opposite: The occasion was hailed as the Wedding of the Year and cheering crowds lining the route to their reception were held back by mounted policemen.

Clementine, shown here in c.1909 with her eldest daughter Diana, undoubtedly
loved her children but struggled to bond with them in the early years.

attentions of Mary Paget, one of Lady Blanche's friends; while in Winston's case, it was nanny Mrs Everest whose unconditional love was the only thing that made him feel safe. Like Clementine, he craved comfort and protection and marriage allowed him to regress to the security of Mrs Everest's nursery, to be folded like an infant within a woman's comforting embrace.

Clementine's pregnancy made Winston's bachelor apartment in Bolton Street impracticable. Tall and narrow with endless flights of stairs and a jumble of military paraphenalia, it was no place to make her first real home anyway. In early 1909, they bought a lease on 33 Eccleston Square in Pimlico, which Clementine decorated in her own trademark pared-down style. She also insisted on having her own bedroom from an early stage. They kept different hours, she preferring to rise early and he to retire late. Winston, moreover, was quickly made to observe the 'protocol of the bedchamber': Clementine needed refuge from her husband's 'dominating brilliance', so he was allowed entry to her room by invitation only.[2]

Their daughter, Diana, was born at home on 11 July and, although it was not yet customary for fathers to attend the actual birth, Winston was at least nearby.

'After four almost any afternoon Miss Churchill receives,'[3] he wrote proudly from his desk at the Board of Trade.

Clementine, however, was feeling neglected and doubtful about her own capacity to fulfil the 'sacred' role of being Mrs Winston Churchill. The minute she was allowed out of bed, she deserted her husband and newborn baby, fleeing to a cottage near Brighton for ten days with Nellie. It appears that in her distress she did not even consider breastfeeding Diana, a task delegated to a wet nurse in London. Winston was left to supervise care of the baby.

Clementine recognised that she could never hope to wrest Winston away from politics by abandoning him. Her sole course of action, if she wanted their marriage to work, was to join him in his 'trade' and she determined to throw herself into his world – indeed, she found politics absorbing. Her letters from this period, on the rare occasions she did leave town, dealt only briefly with Diana's welfare before moving swiftly onto Winston's career. 'I see the Board of Trade Return states that English Industries have improved since last year,' she wrote in October 1909. 'I hope you will bring this out strongly in one of the speeches.'[4] Winston's work was infinitely more alluring than being cooped up with a tiny baby.

·

Clementine needed refuge from her husband's 'dominating brilliance', so he was allowed entry to her room by invitation only.

·

As she threw
herself into politics,
Clementine developed
an astute judgement
of the characters
involved, the goals to
be achieved and the
dangers ahead

As the couple grew accustomed to matrimony, Clementine's explosive temper was frequently unleashed. The slightest setback, such as cold soup or a late delivery, could send her into a fury. Happily, the storm would soon pass with the help of Winston's understanding and patience; 'cast care aside' he would say consolingly. But then he, too, was often impossible to live with – even if he rarely directed his own notorious temper at her.

Although they were evidently much in love (unusually for the time, even holding hands in public), the difference in their political views was also clear. The female vote was just the first of many issues on which Clementine disagreed with Winston. Yet at the same time she was fiercely protective of her husband; when, in 1909, a suffragette lunged at him with a dog whip on the platform at Bristol station, pushing him towards a moving train, Clementine leapt over the piles of luggage and pulled him back with all her might, almost certainly saving his life. Despite that attack, her belief in women's suffrage never faltered.

As she threw herself into politics, Clementine developed an astute judgement of the characters involved, the goals to be achieved and the dangers ahead, and she soon learned how to advance her views with her husband through subtle but effective means. She was thrilled by Winston's work with the Chancellor, David Lloyd George, on providing labour exchanges and workers' pensions and on improving working conditions, and urged him to do more. Yet she foresaw, perhaps before Winston himself, that Lloyd George's radical 'People's Budget' of 1909 – which raised taxes on cars, petrol and land to pay for the foundations of the welfare state – would make politics 'very bitter'. She nevertheless viewed it as heroic to be denigrated for helping the poor, and exulted in watching Winston's popularity with the working classes soar as a result. If he wavered, Clementine was there to stiffen his spine and act as his radical conscience. 'Do not let the glamour or elegance… of old associations blind you,' she warned. Real Tories 'are ignorant, vulgar, prejudiced. They can't bear the idea of the lower classes being independent & free.'[5]

The general election of 1910 was the first of fifteen campaigns Winston and Clementine would fight together, and in which she took an active role. He held his seat in Dundee – perhaps helped a little by Clementine's Scottish ancestry – but overall the Liberals scraped just two more seats than the Conservatives. The new government saw thirty-five-year-old Winston promoted to become the youngest home secretary since Robert Peel.

Clementine became a constant companion to Winston, whether watching him from the gallery in the Commons or as here, escorting him to the law courts.

His workload was onerous, as Prime Minister Herbert Asquith also often delegated to him the job of winding up major debates. So Clementine would sometimes be sent to the 'fighting front' to deliver speeches on her husband's behalf. Pushing the boundaries of what was considered strictly proper for a gentlewoman, she energetically toured labour exchanges and prisons, and gave away prizes at police sports days.

By the time of a second election, called in December 1910 to decide the issue of the reform of the House of Lords, and narrowly won by the Liberals, Clementine was pregnant with their second child. The new baby was due in mid-May 1911 but kept his mother hanging on for another two long weeks. Always anxious during pregnancy, Clementine found the wait unendurable. When Randolph finally put in an appearance, he was immediately granted more attention than his elder sister. While she recuperated, Clementine took

•

Pushing the boundaries of what was considered
strictly proper for a gentlewoman, she energetically
toured labour exchanges and prisons, and gave
away prizes at police sports days.

•

Clementine as usual looking the part at a fox-hunting meet at Blenheim Palace,
the home of Winston's cousin, the Duke of Marlborough.

Randolph and Diana out of London – not to Blenheim or Alderley, but to the scene of her impoverished youth in Seaford. She returned to London in late June 1911 for the coronation of George V, whose father, Edward VII, had died the previous year.

Clementine was becoming more accustomed to Winston's own absences and more tolerant of his work. Now that she had dutifully produced a son and joined forces with her husband in political battle, her self-confidence was growing. Aware that she was now a woman of consequence, she was intent on living up to the part. Her brother, Bill, confessed to Winston that he held her in 'an awe which no one else can rival'.[6] Now widely recognised as a considerable beauty (the artist Neville Lytton comparing her to 'the reincarnation of Venus'), Clementine's social cachet grew still further in October 1911 when Winston became First Lord of the Admiralty. She took up hunting, earning herself a fearless reputation in the saddle. She launched battleships with regal grace. One of Churchill's political rivals, Labour's Ramsay MacDonald, now dubbed her 'queen of wives'.

She also demonstrated extraordinary courage in her official duties. In February 1912, the government was intent on advancing the cause of Irish Home Rule against fierce opposition from Unionists. Ireland teetered on the brink of civil war, and Clementine became fearful for Winston's safety as he prepared for a trip to Belfast. Yet, pregnant for the third time, she insisted on accompanying her husband, despite warnings that she would be putting herself at 'considerable risk'. On the Churchills' arrival, hostile loyalist crowds pressed menacingly up against their car, lifting it from the ground and hurling abuse at its occupants. Although in the end the couple were whisked to relative safety in a Catholic stronghold and Winston was able to deliver his speech, it was a terrifying episode and may have contributed to the miscarriage Clementine suffered in the following month.

It was becoming ever more apparent how Winston relied on his wife. On returning from a jaunt, his first question would always be 'Where's Clemmie?' She began to sense her value to him. Even when he was away, she would attend his social events on her own, speaking to the right people for him and usually saying the right things. With time, it became quite normal for her to sit in on his most important and sensitive discussions. She also began reading his speeches before he delivered them, sometimes suggesting that he cut passages she considered elaborate or harsh. Equally, he was thrilled when she found much to praise, such as when he allowed himself to show emotion and

Above: Clementine playing golf for a parliamentary ladies team. Later she was to use her skills on the fairway to lobby Prime Minister Asquith on Winston's behalf.

Above: Clementine wears an eye-catching outfit to accompany her husband to the launch of HMS *Iron Duke* in October 1912. She was already becoming a style icon.

Opposite: Clementine with Winston (centre) and General Bruce Hamilton during army manoeuvres in Aldershot in 1910. It was highly unusual for a wife to be present at such events but Clementine was constantly breaking the mould.

sympathy. For all his later global fame for oratory, Winston had long since found public speaking an ordeal. Often Clementine would sit in the public gallery at the Commons, smiling encouragingly if he struggled.

In summer 1914, five months into another pregnancy, Clementine took the children, their nanny and a maid to Overstrand, a fashionable Norfolk resort on the east coast of England. She spent an unusually long time with Diana and Randolph, reporting to Winston, 'You will be surprised to hear that they are getting quite fond of me.'[7]

It was otherwise a deeply worrying period. On 28 June 1914, the gunshot in Sarajevo that killed Archduke Franz Ferdinand, heir to the Austro-Hungarian throne, had triggered the events culminating in the outbreak of the First World War. At the time, Clementine was dismayed to be expecting her child in exile, removed from the feverish buzz of London, envious of how her husband was living a thrilling life 'to the tips of your fingers', as she wrote to him. To appease his wife's thirst for news, Winston occasionally took the risk of sending her classified information about the mounting tensions on the Continent. Then, on 4 August, with the great powers of Europe ranged against each other, Britain declared war.[8]

•

It was becoming ever more apparent how
Winston relied on his wife. On returning from a jaunt,
his first question would always be 'Where's Clemmie?'

•

The Pain and the Pride

1914–15

Overstrand was on open coastline, vulnerable to attack.
But while other holidaymakers were packing up, Clementine
found her options curtailed when the local cinema screen
flashed up the message: 'Visitors! Why are you leaving?
Mrs Winston Churchill and her children are in residence...
If it's safe enough for her, surely it's safe enough for you!'
Whatever her inward fears, Clementine could only see it
as her duty to stay put.

Clementine read prodigiously to be able to keep
up with her husband on politics, biography,
history and philosophy.

With hindsight, it is astonishing that Winston failed to bring his family back to London as soon as war broke out. Within months, the eastern seaboard of Britain began to suffer German naval bombardment, and with it considerable loss of life. Perhaps he told himself that Clementine was coping; outwardly she appeared as calm and determined as ever. Or maybe he thought it better that she was out of London, which was beset with fears of Zeppelin bombing raids. In any case, he was engrossed in running the greatest fighting force of the world's greatest empire; Clementine and the children were out of sight and mostly out of mind. It took Nellie finally to reveal that Clementine was approaching hysteria.

Both sisters had considered it too dangerous for Lady Blanche to remain in Dieppe and so Nellie was dispatched to France to bring her back to Overstrand. The family car having broken down, Clementine was now trapped in Norfolk with two little children and a 'taxing' mother, fearful of German attack, her hopes of rejoining her husband dashed. Unable to sleep and heavily pregnant, she became overwrought. Shortly afterwards, she appears to have lost control and even to have attempted self-harm.

'It is absurd to savage myself and to knock my head against the wall,' she scribbled later in a heart-wrenching note to Winston. 'I feel bruised all over and as if I had walked 20 miles and nobody loved me.'[1] Winston's response to what appears to have been some sort of breakdown is not recorded; perhaps, however, her obvious distress finally prompted him to bring her back to London. Clementine returned with the children shortly afterwards for the last few weeks of her pregnancy. Once she was by Winston's side again, she could happily devote herself to his welfare and career; almost immediately, it was as if she were an entirely different woman.

As soon as she arrived back at Admiralty House, Winston's grandiose official residence, Clementine became intimately involved in the conflict. When the Navy won a major battle in late August 1914, it was she who sent word to the War Secretary, Lord Kitchener. She set a precedent by

Opposite: Winston and Clementine brave the English seaside. She favoured low-key holidays such as this, while he preferred luxurious sojourns in the south of France.

accompanying Winston to such male conventions as the inspection of battleships, and she would personally congratulate admirals on their victories, rewarding them with invitations to lunch. Winston briefed her so thoroughly on naval operations that she became better informed than most of the Cabinet.

Clementine's perspicacity contrasted with Winston's rash emotionalism. As First Lord of the Admiralty, he was charged with winning the war at sea, but as a trained soldier with battle experience, he could not help involving himself in affairs on land as well, and he began crossing the Channel regularly to meet with Sir John French, the Commander-in-Chief of the British Expeditionary Force. Aware that Winston always wanted to be at the centre of any major military decision but that others found his 'relish for warmaking'[2] repellent, Clementine was sufficiently astute to see that while his courage was commendable, such conduct made him vulnerable to accusations of adventuring. Her cool analysis – and advice on how to win around his suspicious colleagues – compared tellingly with Winston's own dangerous impulsiveness.

Having gone into labour late on the night of 6 October 1914, Clementine gave birth in the early hours, not to another boy as she had fervently hoped, but to a red-haired daughter who was named Sarah Millicent Hermione. By now, as she later recalled to Pamela Digby, her future daughter-in-law, she had 'decided to give her life totally' to Winston.[3] War had helped Clementine to rediscover her sense of purpose – and it was not as a mother.

The conflict dragged on, and Winston continued to confide in Clementine his hopes, fears and frustrations. She became well-versed in the machinations of the War Council as it struggled to come up with ways of breaking the trench-bound stalemate on the Western Front. Often the only woman at high-level dinners when the most grisly news was discussed, she observed just how many of Winston's colleagues were lacking in energy or ideas. So when he decided to support a seemingly more hopeful plan to the east, Clementine readily familiarised herself with the details. It entailed capturing Constantinople (now Istanbul) by taking control of the Dardanelles Straits, between the Turkish mainland and the Gallipoli peninsula. The idea was to weaken Germany's firepower by eliminating its new ally, Turkey, and creating a direct link to Britain's struggling ally, Russia. Clementine took great interest in the personalities involved, recognising the danger in Winston's appointment of the volatile Admiral Lord Fisher as First Sea Lord. Whereas

War had helped Clementine to rediscover her sense
of purpose – and it was not as a mother.

an infatuated Winston saw in Fisher technical brilliance and devotion to the Navy, Clementine registered truculence, a volcanic temper and a genius bordering on madness.

Fisher's erratic changes of opinion about the viability of the Dardanelles plan served only to confirm Clementine's doubts, while his wavering did nothing to improve the quality of its preparations. From the start, the forces were ill-equipped: on the eve of departure, one key battalion lacked doctors and drugs. Here, for the first time, Clementine demonstrated her extraordinary skill at high-level organisation, personally arranging for the necessary 'details' to be picked up en route at Malta.[4] Naval bombardment started on 19 February 1915 and initial progress was good. Then, unaccountably, after the loss of a handful of Allied ships, the admirals ordered the fleet to withdraw, thereby providing the hard-pressed Turks with the chance to replenish their depleted stocks of ammunition. When the Army was sent in to launch amphibious landings in April of that year, it encountered ferocious fire, resulting in huge loss of life. Kitchener, the initial advocate of the plan, effectively killed the whole offensive by refusing to send more troops.

This appalling mess of ineptitude, resulting in more than 200,000 British casualties alone, was the work of many, and yet a single scapegoat would suffice. Winston was still seen as a traitor by the Tories, having an insufferable ego by the Liberals, untrustworthy by the King and a blood-smeared hothead by voters, the obvious choice, he was held liable for one of the bloodiest British military failures of all time. Clementine would have to endure the name 'Gallipoli' shouted at her husband as a term of abuse, for decades to come. Yet her loyalty never faltered; nor did her sense of outrage.[6] She held Prime Minister Asquith responsible for Winston's demise in his desperate bid to save his own skin.

In truth, she and Asquith were opposed in temperament and never saw eye to eye. There was some veracity in his view of Clementine: she was critical, reserved and could be prudish. Clementine had long been genuinely shocked that 'Old Squiffy', even in wartime, continued his boozy social rounds, while a generation of young men was slaughtered. While he had been a great peacetime social reformer, Asquith no longer seemed concerned for the poor, nor did he change gear to deal headlong with the catastrophe befalling his country in times of war. No wonder Clementine railed against such a man throwing Winston to the wolves.

> Clementine would have to endure the name 'Gallipoli' shouted at her husband as a term of abuse, for decades to come.

Clementine accompanies Winston to Hendon Air Pageant in 1914. He adored flying at this point in his life – he went off it later – but Clementine found his frequent sorties into the skies deeply alarming because of the all too frequent plane crashes in the early days of aviation.

•

Despite the terrible likelihood that her husband would be killed or maimed if he went to the Front, Clementine remained admirably calm, organised, even cheerful throughout. She seemed fortified by an unshakeable conviction that he was preordained for greatness, and that this was merely another stage in his journey.

•

Opposite: Winston and Clementine taking a stroll in 1914. Both are wearing striking headwear, but Winston had a much larger collection of hats than his wife.

Upon his removal from the Admiralty at the end of May 1915, Winston was given the nebulous post of Chancellor of the Duchy of Lancaster in the new coalition government. His isolation – political and social – was complete. Further humiliation for both Churchills came when he was excluded from the newly formed War Council. Those few still close to him believed that it was only his marriage that saved him from self-destruction, the darkness of his moods frightening them. General Hastings 'Pug' Ismay, Winston's chief of staff during the Second World War, was convinced that only Clementine's unbreakable loyalty preserved Winston's 'sanity' in the First: she was 'his rock during that terrible time'.[5]

Not only had Winston been kicked out of power, the Churchills' household had also been shorn of its trappings, including a roof over their heads in London. Winston spent many nights with his mother at 72 Brook Street, Mayfair, while in mid-June, Clementine and the children went to live with his brother and sister-in-law, Jack and Goonie, at 41 Cromwell Road, South Kensington. But Winston, restless as ever, had been considering a return to soldiering, and now resolved that if he was to be prevented from waging the war at his desk in London, he would fight it on the frontline. He would take up his commission as a major in the Oxfordshire Hussars and rejoin his regiment in France. On 11 November 1915, he wrote to Asquith resigning from his government post in order to place himself at the 'disposal of the military authorities'.[6]

Despite the terrible likelihood that her husband would be killed or maimed if he went to the Front, Clementine remained admirably calm, organised, even cheerful throughout. She seemed fortified by an unshakeable conviction that he was preordained for greatness, and that this was merely another stage in his journey. She was a woman with conviction; one who knew her worth in a true partnership.

I Believe in Your Star

1915–16

Major Winston Churchill arrived in Boulogne, northern
France, on 18 November 1915. His reception with champagne
and a hot bath at General Headquarters in St Omer befitted
his former VIP status as a senior politician and also his
own sense of importance. But it sat uncomfortably with
the new reality of being a middle-ranking officer bound
for the trenches.

Churchill was widely blamed in 1915 for the
Gallipoli disaster, but Clementine remained
his most stalwart supporter and helped to
rehabilitate his career.

The Churchill family at Admiralty House in 1915. From left to right: Winston Churchill, his daughter,
Diana, Clementine with the newborn Sarah, Randolph, his mother Lady Randolph,
Lady Gwendoline Churchill with her two sons, and Winston's brother, Jack.

W inston could have remained there in the well-appointed Château de Blendecques, but both he and Clementine knew that – save for personal safety – there would be little benefit for him in a staff post at GHQ. Within a few days, he was at the Front, with its stinking mud, bloated rats and rotting corpses, although he talked down the dangers to Clementine, insisting that there was 'nothing to complain about … except cold feet'.[1]

This did not mean he intended to tolerate unnecessary hardships. Clementine found herself frantically busy supplying lists of urgently required (but often scarce) items, such as periscopes, sheepskin sleeping bags, small face towels, trench wading boots, leather waistcoats, beefsteak pies and chocolate. Regularly, she would send him hampers of carefully chosen delicacies, which he shared around his fellow officers, prompting raucous cheers for Clementine in her absence. Indeed, Winston reported on 19 November, 'I am very happy here … I did not know what release from care meant.'[2]

For Clementine, left at home to march alone, there was no corresponding sense of escape. After seven years at the centre of power, she missed the hubbub of political life. She did not enjoy Winston's previous status or his access to high-level information. Women had not yet achieved the vote, there were no female MPs and when they were permitted to visit the House of Commons to watch parliamentary debates, they had to do so from the Ladies' Gallery. Her gender restricted what Clementine could do, and yet studying politics – and politicians – at Winston's side had imbued her with a sense of who mattered and what to say to them.

Fortunately, she drew intense pride from Winston's courage in willingly suffering the horrors of trench warfare; she also soon recognised that it was working wonders for his reputation. His new 'military halo', as she called it, gave her a glimmer of hope for his future rehabilitation as a national figure and so, when not scouring London's shops for his creature comforts, she set about what amounted to a full-on 'Bring Back Winston' campaign, long before the term 'lobbying' had been invented. Engineering lunches with Cabinet ministers to plead her husband's case, she also courted newspaper editors, dealt with daily press enquiries and sent Winston all his cuttings. She understood the potency of *his* celebrity, while she avoided giving much of *herself* away to journalists. It was an approach she would maintain for the rest of her life.

•

Her gender restricted what Clementine could do, and yet studying politics – and politicians – at Winston's side had imbued her with a sense of who mattered and what to say to them.

•

There is at this time surprisingly little in Clementine's letters to Winston about their children, Diana, Randolph and Sarah. Clementine loved them and was 'devoted to their welfare', but the whole focus of her life and her emotions was out there in France. Very occasionally, she would mention how Diana's new haircut made her look like Peter Pan, that Sarah was 'on the verge of voluble speech' or how Randolph was showing a precocious interest in the war. She wrote more frequently, however, about her concerns over Winston's health, fretting that he was not inoculated against typhoid and waking in the night from nightmares of him shivering in the cold. Perhaps Clementine's greatest worry, however, was how to prevent her impetuous husband from damaging his political prospects further. She could not have been more opposed, for instance, to Winston's kneejerk desire for immediate and unsuitable preferment from Field Marshal French – a divergence of views that would generate a great deal of heat between them. Understanding clearly that Winston's best interests lay in staying at the Front and being seen to rise up the ranks by merit, she was forthright in her assertion that only in this way could he begin to repair the damage done to his reputation back home. She understood the importance of her husband's public image far more than he did.

Indeed, her courage in standing up to Winston is remarkable. Forceful, impatient and loquacious, he dominated those around him; it was difficult for almost anyone, however powerful or self-assured, to withstand the full force of his invective. Whenever Clementine lost face-to-face, she would re-marshal her arguments in writing. However exhausting the fight, she would rarely give up. This refusal to cede ground on important matters persisted throughout their marriage and was one of Clementine's most conspicuous traits.

•

Winston came home on leave for Christmas 1915; it was a welcome family get-together and reprieve from the strains of the past few weeks. He stayed at Cromwell Road, where Clementine and the children were still living, for just a long weekend, and, making use of the opportunity to see his political contacts, he had very little time alone with his wife. It seems that she found him attractive in uniform, though. Having had to run with him for his train back to the Front, Clementine recalled being out of breath and unable to speak at the time, but she wrote to him later: 'I could not tell you how much I wanted you at the station.'[3] It is probably the most explicit note between them that survives.

Although exhausted after the frantic activity of Winston's short visit, Clementine returned to the work of restoring his reputation the day after his departure by inviting Asquith's great rival, Lloyd George, to lunch at Cromwell Road. In a meeting that Clementine found a great strain, Lloyd George uttered all the right things, saying repeatedly, 'We must get Winston back,' but she found herself incapable of believing him. So she decided to swallow her pride and 'reconnoitre Downing Street'; she would skilfully

Opposite: Dressed in pure white, Clementine cut a conspicuous figure when Winston addressed a crowd at the Enfield Lock Munition Works in 1915. His audiences came to expect her presence.

deploy all her charms to woo the Asquiths instead, with the intention of re-establishing the 'civil relations' damaged by Winston's sacking. Believing she was getting the measure of the Prime Minister, she begged Winston not to do anything that might jeopardise her progress.

As well as looking after Winston's interests, Clementine had been spearheading, since the first German gas attack back in April, a national appeal to housewives to help make emergency gas masks for the Front – the first time a woman had ever undertaken such a role. In June, she had also gone back to work organising canteens for munitions workers. Over the next few months, she took on responsibility for opening, staffing and running nine refectories across north London, each feeding up to 500 workers at a time. Although she had no previous experience in managing anything beyond the household, she turned out to be extremely effective.

Clementine's new position of authority gave her the chance to advance her feminist beliefs. In a small but significant step towards sexual equality, she introduced a rule that women workers could smoke in the same rest areas as their male colleagues. The thousands of women for the first time employed in heavy industry fascinated her. Socially, Clementine still mixed exclusively with her own class, but her obvious concern for the less fortunate and her unusual dedication to their welfare distinguished her from other upper-class women drafted in to help with the war effort. Despite her aristocratic origins, Clementine's relatively impoverished childhood and brief experience of work had also fostered in her an instinctive sympathy for the worker's point of view. It was an understanding that would serve her well in the years to come.

•

The apocalyptic stalemate on the Western Front was to see the loss, by the end of 1915, of 285,000 men. In December, the evacuation of the Dardanelles began, countless more lives having been wasted. The disastrous failures of the two campaigns had prompted a massive fall in public support for the war, yet the need for men was greater than ever. Conscription was introduced in January 1916.

Clementine's charm offensive with the Asquiths was going well, however, and in mid-February she was invited to spend a weekend with them at their

•

She had given him her love, wisdom and counsel but
he was a man possessed, unwilling to listen.

•

country residence. Asquith resolutely refused to discuss the war, even as they heard the boom of shellfire from across the Channel. She nevertheless gauged from their conversations that he was still fond of Winston and would like him back in the government. On 25 February, she raised the stakes by issuing an invitation to dinner at her house. She knew success depended on securing eight acceptable, amusing bridge players for the Prime Minister's 'comfort & happiness'. After working 'like a beaver' on this and every other aspect of the evening, she was able to proclaim the event a triumph. The 'old sybarite thoroughly enjoyed himself' and the Churchill family 'presented a solid & prosperous appearance', she wrote to Winston. She made sure to sit next to Asquith himself and he duly went home some time later in 'high good humour'.[4]

Winston was granted leave in early March. He was now being urged by several associates – most of whom Clementine thought 'wrong-headed' – to give up soldiering and return to politics. When supporters urged him to lead an attack on the government over its patent mismanagement of the war, Clementine's protestations were to no avail. He decided to make a dramatic intervention in a Commons debate on naval spending – a move that jeopardised all Clementine's painstaking work to ease his eventual return to high office. At first, the speech went quite well, as he made a powerful and valid case against the Navy's inactivity. But then, disregarding all of Clementine's counsel, he called for Lord Fisher, who as a prime mover in the Dardanelles catastrophe had been the chief architect of his downfall, to be reappointed First Sea Lord. The result of this unfathomable move was the loss of any residual parliamentary support.

In the ensuing furore, Clementine had hardly any time alone with Winston before his departure a week later from Dover to the Front. She longed for him to come back, she wrote to him on 13 March, but only when he would be 'welcomed & acclaimed by all'.[5] She knew that, should he stay in the trenches, 'a wicked bullet' might well find him and yet, in a letter dated 6 April, she made one last attempt to persuade him to stay, an effort that confirms the acuity of her political sense. 'To be great one's actions must be able to be understood by simple people. Your motive for going to the Front was easy to understand – Your motive for coming back requires explanation.'[6]

She had given him her love, wisdom and counsel but he was a man possessed, unwilling to listen. A few weeks later, Winston was back in London for good.

Opposite: Clementine and Winston accompanied by Admiral Hood (centre, left) during a visit to Lords Cricket Ground in 1916.

Loss Unimaginable

1916–22

With Winston's return from the trenches, uninjured, in May 1916, Clementine's life was transformed. He immediately set about his rehabilitation with the public with her guidance. Lloyd George had finally manoeuvred Asquith out of power in December 1916, following the disastrous Somme offensive. But, even after the fall of his nemesis, Winston remained untouchable. His one-time political twin fought shy of bringing him into the new government in even the most junior role. Deliverance came following the publication, in March 1917, of the preliminary findings of the Dardanelles Commission, which partly exonerated Winston. Three weeks later, the US entered the war; Lloyd George now badly needed a minister of munitions with energy, efficiency and imagination. When in July, he decided to hand the appointment to Winston, it was just what Clementine had hoped for.

Clementine with Marigold, her third daughter, who died in tragic circumstances in 1921 when only two years old. Her mother never forgave herself for her death and barely spoke of the little girl again.

Winston's new office triggered a by-election in his Dundee constituency. While he ecstatically plunged into his new war work, Clementine took over much of the campaigning. The Churchill name inevitably attracted a lot of barracking, but Clementine gamely dealt with the hecklers while lending a compassionate ear to their complaints. In large part thanks to her efforts, Winston was returned with a sizeable majority.

Thereafter, Clementine's new home in Eccleston Square quickly became an alternative nerve centre for the war, with ministers and messengers coming and going all day and night and secretaries pounding away on typewriters. Now he was back in the saddle, Winston's state of mind was positively joyful. But a buoyant Winston was also a selfish and dictatorial one. Clementine had shared his humiliation and helped him to absolution, but now her wishes were largely ignored. After she became pregnant for the fifth time in early 1918, she was distressed by his frequent trips to the Front. She was so consumed by dread and foreboding that she could not stop herself pouring out her fears in front of her bewildered children.

He also refused to live within their means. Lullenden, the Churchills' new country retreat in Surrey, where the children had been sent in the summer of 1917, away from the air raids in London, was proving costly to run. Once Winston was back at work, its management fell to Clementine. Her cousin, Madeline Whyte, rented a cottage nearby for a month to help out, but Clementine was succumbing to anxiety and exhaustion.

She was frightened to be with child again in the spring of 1918. Aged thirty-three, pregnancy exhausted her, made her feel neurotic, and threatened to strand her in the country because she had no fixed abode in London. She despaired at the thought of another baby on the way when she already found her existing children so challenging. Since her early excitement at having produced a son, her feelings towards Randolph had cooled, making her doubt her abilities as a mother. The children had been left largely to their own devices at Lullenden, and unrestrained by either his adoring father or his concerned but distant mother, Randolph was becoming distinctly unruly: on one occasion he had even instigated the emptying of a chamber pot on the head of Lloyd George, a regular visitor to the house. Now Clementine feared that she might be carrying twins, with all the expense and worry that would entail. It lingered in the back of her mind that she would be found wanting by her husband; she knew too well how often men exploited their wives'

•

At the end of 1918, in recognition of her efforts, she was
made a Commander of the Order of the British Empire
(CBE). It was a great honour and gave notice to all those
doubters and critics that, given the chance, she could be
much more than a powerful man's ornament.

•

pregnancies as 'excuses' for conducting affairs. But perhaps worst of all was
the idea that Winston's political resurgence and the restrictions imposed by
her condition might make her redundant as his counsellor-in-chief.

It is thus perhaps a little surprising that she did not abandon her canteen
work at this difficult stage. She continued to drive herself extremely hard
and the canteens were the only part of Clementine's life that were her own.
At the end of 1918, in recognition of her efforts, she was made a Commander
of the Order of the British Empire (CBE). It was a great honour and gave
notice to all those doubters and critics that, given the chance, she could be
much more than a powerful man's ornament.

Clementine was now particularly keen to make sure that the women who
had contributed so much towards the war effort would not be abandoned.
With Winston's public image, as ever, at the forefront of her mind, she
perceived the need for him to rebadge himself a social reformer. The world
outside had changed forever. Total war had brought about a social revolution.
British society was never to be quite so unequal again and women were no
longer seen as hysterical weaklings. Earlier in the war, the Speaker of the
House of Commons, James William Lowther, had chaired a conference on
electoral reform that had recommended limited women's suffrage. When, in
early 1918, it was proposed to grant the vote to property-owning women over
thirty, Clementine doggedly persuaded her husband to vote for the changes,
but Winston was prepared to go only so far on female emancipation. In 1919,
when Nancy Astor became the first woman to sit as an MP, he was among a
number of men who blanked her despite having known her for years.

By the autumn of 1918, when Clementine was enduring the final months of her pregnancy, it seemed that victory in war was in sight. The conflict had dominated the Churchills' lives for more than four years, testing both their marriage and their sanity, making them social and political pariahs and driving them to virtual bankruptcy. But by its end, Winston had proven himself a resourceful, innovative and driven minister and had won the respect of many of his critics. Under Clementine's influence, his reputation had undergone a remarkable recovery.

Clementine wanted badly to be with him when the Armistice finally came. Minutes before eleven o'clock on Monday 11 November, she ran excitedly into his office off Trafalgar Square. Outside there was a strange but expectant silence. Then, just as they heard the strokes of Big Ben, they saw through the windows a solitary office girl come down into the street. Soon there were hundreds pouring out of doors or leaning out of windows, cheering and waving. Within minutes the roads were full of smiling faces. Elated by the scene, Winston ordered a car and as he and Clementine climbed inside they were surrounded by well-wishers. It had been so long since the couple had been cheered rather than booed – now at last they were experiencing together the joy of being hailed as heroes.

Just four days later, on 15 November 1918, Clementine gave birth to a red-haired girl named Marigold. Even without the feared complications of twins, it was a difficult delivery, and mother and baby both suffered. Marigold was just ten days old when Parliament was dissolved and a new election announced. Fortunately, for once, Clementine was not dragooned into electioneering; the result was all but a foregone conclusion. Triumphant in war, Lloyd George's coalition secured a massive victory at the polls. For all his bellicose reputation, Winston actually swam against the tide in speaking out against calls for harsh treatment of Germany, making Clementine very proud of what she considered a true manifestation of his liberal beliefs.

After a lavish Christmas at Blenheim, Winston started work in January 1919 at the War Office. Lloyd George had made him both Secretary of State

for War and Secretary of State for Air. In the meantime, he allowed himself to relax and enjoy the splendours of Blenheim at Yuletide. Clementine endured the overwhelmingly Churchillian celebrations for Winston's sake, but the forbidding grandeur of Blenheim still offended her Liberal sensibility. She was also nervous about the future. Although his new job came with £5,000 a year, her antennae had already detected discontent about Winston's bagging of two senior positions. As before, his many duties frequently took him away to France and elsewhere. Clementine was extremely put out by his absences. A letter to Winston, written after their eleventh wedding anniversary, however, offers an insight into what it was that kept her in such a challenging marriage: 'My Darling, you have been the great event in [my life]. You took me from the straitened little by-path I was treading and took me with you into the life & colour & jostle of the high-way.'[1]

In 1921, Winston was moved to the Colonial Office. Having hoped to become Chancellor of the Exchequer, he was bitterly disappointed by this turn of events. Moreover, in early 1919 the Churchills were without a permanent London home or the means to procure one, something that caused Clementine great distress. Unlike the Admiralty, neither the War

Office nor Winston's appointment as Colonial Secretary brought with them official residences, and their financial straits were such that Winston had been forced to sell Lullenden – although, as if oblivious to Clementine's emotional state, he was already instructing agents to find him another country seat in his favoured county of Kent. With a newborn baby and three other small children, Clementine had to endure a merry-go-round of temporary and often unsuitable abodes mostly rented from friends or extended family.

In January 1921, however, Clementine and Winston had finally taken their first holiday together since before the outbreak of the war. Although only thirty-six, Clementine was neither physically nor emotionally robust and she increasingly questioned whether she had enough energy or strength to sustain her stressful lifestyle. Their escape to a hotel in Nice in the south of France

Below: Clementine and Winston take Sarah to the Mall in London to watch troops of the Brigade of Guards in a march past. 22 January 1919.

Although only thirty-six, Clementine was neither physically nor emotionally robust and she increasingly questioned whether she had enough energy or strength to sustain her stressful lifestyle.

•

came as a welcome tonic. Yet even this was not to be an intimate break alone. They had barely unpacked their suitcases before Winston was called back to London.

Perhaps such separations helped to keep their relationship fresh; Clementine certainly tried to adopt a philosophical approach when they occurred. But they also sometimes left her feeling isolated, even abandoned. Time was slipping by so fast and she was struggling to reconcile herself to the fact that she was approaching middle age. So, when Winston went back to London, Clementine stayed on in France.

Then, at the end of January, a distant cousin of Winston's was killed in a railway accident. As he was childless, his Irish estate and a large pile of cash went to Winston. This unexpected windfall had the potential to net him some £4,000 a year, almost as much as the salary he received as a minister. Even Clementine, constitutionally insecure about their finances, could now look forward to a more 'carefree' future.

Winston's appointment as Colonial Secretary also brought the prospect of exciting travel. One of the first trips involved a conference on Middle Eastern affairs in Cairo and he suggested Clementine join him on board ship straight from her extended holiday in the south of France. Undeterred by the fact that she had not seen her children for nigh on two months, she was thrilled at her first chance to accompany Winston on official business abroad. At Winston's

Clementine attends an inspection of the Royal
Naval Division of the Horse Guards in 1919 with
Winston and Lieutenant Bruce Ashcroft.

Clementine (far left in white) visited the pyramids on camelback in 1921 with a party that included Winston (on her left), Gertrude Bell (third from left) and T.E. Lawrence (fourth from left).

Clementine loved to travel with Winston on his official business, even when dangerous or uncomfortable. Here she is with him (to the right at the front) at a Government House reception in Jerusalem, Palestine, in March 1921.

side, Clementine glowed with a fresh vitality. The glamorous T.E. Lawrence – Lawrence of Arabia – joined them and they became close friends. During the trip, she played tennis – she had become a keen amateur player – met politicians, ambassadors and leading archaeologists, and the Churchills lived and travelled in great luxury. There was even time for magical visits on camelback to the Pyramids of Giza with Lawrence. In such exalted company, Clementine established herself as something of a cool customer, literally – while others sweated and swooned in the heat, she remained unflustered.

Winston had arrived to a wave of hostility and several credible death threats. Even from the safety of the armoured car provided to transport them, the Churchills must have found it unnerving to be met with angry crowds of Egyptian nationalists pelting stones at them. Yet Winston's bodyguard, Walter Thompson, was astonished by Clementine's courage, noting that 'nothing seemed ever to disturb or to dishearten her'.[2]

At the end of the conference, Clementine did not hurry home but spent two leisurely weeks wandering back to England via Alexandria, Sicily and Naples. By the time she finally returned on 10 April, she had been away for a good three months. Rested, fulfilled and happy, she was pleased to be reunited with the children. Randolph, now nearly ten, was grumpy and demanding, and Marigold was suffering from yet another cold, but Clementine was hugely moved that they had all made a 'Welcome Home' banner, which they hoisted as her car drew up outside the house. At such moments, her reserve melted away and she joyfully scooped them up in her arms. If only she could always be so spontaneous. But perhaps this was a new beginning. Winston's career was back on track, she was by his side and she had a secure home at last.

Her contentment was not to last. Four days later, her brother, Bill, was found shot dead in a Paris hotel room. Just thirty-three, he was handsome and charming and had gone into business after retiring from the Navy at the end of the war. Like his mother and his twin sister, Nellie, though, he had a weakness for gambling. Winston had once or twice helped him to cover his losses and had recently made him promise to stop betting on cards. When Bill died, he seemed to have been in funds and had not long ago deposited 10,000 francs into a bank account; even so, it was soon confirmed that he had killed himself.

At the news of his death, Clementine rushed over to her distraught mother in Dieppe, where Lady Blanche had resettled after the war, and took charge.

•

It had been such a grisly six months, yet Clementine was
determined to enjoy her summer. At the beginning of
August, all four children were packed off to seaside lodgings
in Broadstairs, Kent, with yet another new nanny.

•

Clementine loved to watch professional tennis and is here attending the Wimbledon Lawn Champions with Lady Birkenhead in June 1920.

Suicide was not a crime in France at the time, but was a sin in Catholic doctrine and at first it seemed that the family might not be allowed to bury Bill in consecrated ground. Winston pulled strings, however, and the British Vice-Consul was dispatched to put pressure on the local clergyman to accommodate Lady Blanche's desperate wish for a 'decent' funeral. Yet nothing would quite expunge either the shame or the grief of Bill's death. Clementine was frantic to avoid any impression that her only brother was 'a mere scapegrace disowned by his family'. In order to lend the occasion an appropriate grandeur, she delayed the service until late afternoon to make it easier for her husband to attend. Winston dropped everything and dashed across the Channel, arriving just in time.

Two months after Bill's suicide, death visited the Churchills again, when equally unexpectedly, Jennie, Winston's mother, died. After a broken ankle sustained in May 1921 turned to gangrene and the foot had to be amputated, Jennie bore her misfortune and pain with extraordinary fortitude and humour. Though she had never been close to her mother-in-law, Clementine could not fail to be impressed by her courage. Then, early on the morning of 29 June, Jennie suffered a sudden and violent haemorrhage. Winston ran crying through the streets of London in his dressing gown to be with her, but by the time he reached her bedside it was too late.

It had been such a grisly six months, yet Clementine was determined to enjoy her summer. At the beginning of August, all four children were packed off to seaside lodgings in Broadstairs, Kent, with yet another new nanny. In the meantime, Clementine visited the Duke and Duchess of Westminster at their Cheshire stately home, Eaton Hall. Without either Winston, who was working, or the children, she would be blissfully free to relax, socialise and

Clementine dressed for the part even when playing sport. Surbiton, May 1920.

take part in one of her beloved tennis tournaments without the distractions of family life.

The children dutifully wrote to their mother about shrimp-fishing, rowing boats and sunburn. From the beginning though, both Randolph and Sarah also alluded to Marigold being unwell. Her temperature had soared and she began to find it difficult to breathe. Eventually a local doctor was called but his remedies were limited. Only when the terrified landlady of the lodgings absolutely insisted, did the nanny finally call Clementine with the dreaded news that Marigold had developed septicaemia.

Clementine dashed down to Broadstairs as quickly as she could, while the three elder children were dispatched to Scotland with a maid. By the time she arrived, Marigold was in a critical condition. Winston shot down from London soon afterwards and a specialist doctor was summoned. It was all too late, however. Both were with their daughter, when Marigold died the next day, three months short of her third birthday. They buried her in Kensal Green Cemetery on 26 August 1921, and erected a simple, unassuming headstone. It was as if a book had been slammed shut. To the end of her life, Clementine would barely speak of Marigold again.

Clementine made her way wearily back south to London without Winston to prepare the children for the new school term. Somehow she kept going with all the rituals and errands of her life; inside, she would never get over her grief or quite dispel a gnawing sense of guilt.

By the end of that year, Clementine was an emotional and physical wreck. Her deep depression – marked by severe listlessness alternating with near-hysterical outbursts – appears to have been far more serious than Winston's brooding periods of what he called the 'Black Dog'. The doctors were flummoxed as to what to do with her and merely prescribed another vacation.

On Boxing Day, Winston chose to go to the Riviera without Clementine in the company of Prime Minister Lloyd George, happily indulging himself in his normal round of politics, painting, writing and hunting. Clementine was to join them as soon as the school term started. However, luck turned cruelly against her. Within hours of Winston's departure, Diana, Randolph and several servants were struck by a deadly strain of influenza. A few days later, Clementine herself collapsed from nervous exhaustion and the doctor ordered her to bed for a week. By the time she was finally free from sickroom duties and fit to travel, Winston had returned to London. She travelled to Cannes and it was there that her suspicions were confirmed: she was pregnant again.

•

It was as if a book had been slammed shut. To the end of her life, Clementine would barely speak of Marigold again.

•

85

The Churchills arriving at Westminster Abbey for a memorial service for an Admiral in May 1921 during one of the most traumatic periods of their life together.

His mother and daughter's deaths apart, Winston's work at the Colonial Office had also not been free of trouble. The fiercely nationalist Sinn Fein had gone on to win a majority of Irish seats in the 1918 general election and within a matter of weeks they had proclaimed an Irish Republic. The violence of the ensuing war of independence had continued sporadically since. It was a problem in which Clementine took a great interest. The solution was by no means simple – the massive support for Sinn Fein in the south was balanced by that for the Unionists in the north. Nevertheless, Clementine felt sympathy for the Catholics, particularly since they had helped the Churchills escape loyalist mobs during their trip to Belfast in 1912. She consequently pleaded with Winston to ensure 'some sort of justice' in Ireland, and to draw back from 'iron-fisted' or 'Hunnish' treatment of the Irish rebels. And it appears that her pleas for moderation may have softened his approach. He even invited Michael Collins, a key Sinn Fein negotiator, to their home in Sussex Square and devoted much of the second half of 1921 to Irish affairs. The resultant truce was followed by a treaty that would eventually lead to independence for southern Ireland.

In mid-August 1922, Winston decamped to the Duke of Westminster's chateau near Biarritz. So it was that Clementine, finding herself without her husband for the last weeks of her final pregnancy, sought respite at Frinton-on-Sea on the Essex coast. In September, the couple were reunited in London for the birth. Marigold could never be replaced, let alone forgotten, but the new baby would help Clementine to ease the pain. Mary arrived safely early on the morning of 15 September. Winston took advantage of the occasion. It was the one and only time in their marriage that he would betray her trust.

A Chandelier's Life and Sparkle

1922–29

Winston had spotted Chartwell – a former foundling house near Westerham in Surrey dating to the reign of Henry VIII – the previous year. He was seduced by its seclusion and quintessentially English views. When Clementine came to view the house, she was similarly entranced. Doubts soon set in, though. To the south lay a lovely vista, but on the other sides were a steep wooded bank and hordes of light-sucking rhododendrons and laurels. The house itself, moreover, had suffered a ponderous Victorian makeover. Downstairs the rooms were small, dark and mostly faced away from the view, and upstairs was infested with earwigs. Ravaged by damp, it would be ruinous to heat. That, she had thought, was the end of it.

Clementine played tennis whenever she could, even when pregnant. Here she is at the courts in Regent's Park, London, but her dream was to build her own court at Chartwell.

In truth, Chartwell was already his. Winston had allowed her to continue in the belief that the house was unsuitable while behind her back he negotiated a price. When she found out, Clementine was appalled and deeply hurt. Later she was to say that this was the only time in their marriage that Winston was less than candid with her.

While Chartwell was to become the Churchills' principal residence for forty years – and their only long-term home – it would drain their finances and sap her energy. Substantial renovations would be required, which would eventually cost twice the original estimate and take eighteen months to complete. Nevertheless, Clementine accepted she was its new chatelaine with grace, if not enthusiasm, and set about transforming it into a haven.

As the bills for Chartwell started to mount, the coalition government of which Winston was a member was falling apart. Then, on 19 October 1922, days before a general election was called, he was rushed into theatre to have his appendix removed, and was out of action until mid-November. Five weeks after giving birth, Clementine found herself assuming his place on the stump once again. Taking Mary, she made the 500-mile trip to his Scottish constituency for what was to be a bitter campaign. She represented Winston faithfully, despite her private belief that his virulent anti-Labour line was ill-judged. A more heartfelt Liberal than her husband, she was genuinely moved by the deprivation she witnessed on Tayside and could see the appeal the Labour Party held for those who had so little. Yet Winston continued to ignore her pleas to take 'a less hostile and negative' attitude. As she stood defiantly next to him at the count – he had risen from his sick bed to be present – her judgement was confirmed: he came an inglorious fourth.

With builders at work on Chartwell and nothing to detain them in London, Winston and Clementine set off to the south of France. These months away from everyday politics were in many ways idyllic: Clementine was able to

Clementine never really liked Chartwell – she thought it a dark and difficult house – but it became their home for forty years and she turned it into an elegant and comfortable country seat for them both.

practise her tennis, Winston could paint, they celebrated her thirty-eighth birthday in style and he gave her a diamond brooch. The house was always bustling and Winston and Clementine were still rarely alone. Not only did servants accompany them everywhere, but Winston's secretary and researcher were present, too. Even so, this may have been one of the longest periods they spent together in their marriage.

When they returned from France in mid-May 1923, Chartwell was still a mud-splattered building site. For a year they were obliged to rent a place nearby. Chartwell was no Blenheim, but Winston viewed it as a dynastic seat that would eventually pass to Randolph. Clementine much preferred the culture and people of London, but they could no longer afford to keep two large residences. Her beloved home in Sussex Square would have to go, and she was now effectively trapped. When the Churchills finally moved into Chartwell, in 1924, Clementine was absent, having chosen to visit her mother in Dieppe. Normally she took solo charge of domestic arrangements; this time it was she who was running away. Removing herself was always her most powerful weapon. Her antipathy to Chartwell disappointed Winston and her absence wounded him. His physical comfort was provided by a host of staff, but only Clementine's presence engendered deeper feelings of security.

The truth was, however, that Clementine found his dependency on her draining; like a child, he was petulant, moody and demanding. As everyone in the household would discover, being out of office made Winston exceedingly grumpy. And the more childlike he was, the more she felt duty-bound to play the responsible adult. So she devoted herself to running the large house for Winston's pleasure.

Under Clementine's charge, Chartwell took on a simple, comfortable yet stylish air; the house, and particularly its dining room, would become the site of many a weighty political discussion. Her signature style was in evidence almost everywhere, whether in the porcelain blue of her sitting room or the primrose yellows of the drawing room. The carefully positioned mirrors to lighten the gloomy interiors were her inspiration, as were the colourful curtains at the windows. The principal chambers were graced by a sprinkling of good but modest antiques and there were fine French glass (not crystal) chandeliers. She regarded the services of an interior designer a gross extravagance and liked nothing better than to find an attractive piece of furniture going 'for a song'. Flowers from the gardens were placed in every

Opposite: Winston was unwell so Clementine fought the November 1922 election on his behalf in his then Dundee constituency although she disapproved of his 'Smash the Socialists' sentiments. She had given birth just five weeks previously.

•

Under Clementine's charge, Chartwell took on a simple, comfortable yet stylish air; the house, and particularly its dining room, would become the site of many a weighty political discussion.

•

room: 'Grab them by the necks and just drop them in the vase, dear,' she would instruct staff. She could be furious if she found fussy arrangements, and on formal occasions would only countenance white. The wood gleamed and smelt of beeswax, the glassware sparkled, cushions were puffed, the silverware polished, the paintings perfectly aligned in vertical rows.

Maintaining such standards, even with a large staff, took its toll on her nerves. The slightest imperfection could prompt a terrifying putdown. Yet she disliked having 'people around her who were frightened of her'[1] and could also deploy tact and gratitude to equal effect. One of her youthful smiles would reward a job well done. She made the best of a challenging house, and the results of her perfectionism were admired and widely copied.

The only corner of the house immune to Clementine's touch was her husband's bedroom, a swashbuckling shrine to military memorabilia with a single bed. Some distance away was Clementine's far more splendid sky-blue, barrel-domed boudoir, with its imposing four-poster bed dressed in red moiré silk. In summer, white roses from the garden graced her desk, and the windows would be thrown open to capture the fresh air.

The dining room was the focus of Clementine's efforts to keep Winston happy. Heaven help the cook should he or she fail to provide a regular supply of his favourite dishes such as clear soup (never creamy), oysters, pheasant, dressed crab, Dover sole, chocolate éclairs and roast beef and Yorkshire pudding. If she asked what she was expected to feed his guests, his answer was typically Irish stew 'with lots of onions'; or for grander occasions, lobster and roast duck. Winston's preference was for hearty English cooking, and every morning, at half past eight, she would spend a full half-hour in her bedroom discussing the day's meals with the cook to ensure that all was to his taste. Such culinary exactitude masked an ulterior motive. Feeding Winston well was her way, she once confessed, of 'managing' him.

The prospect of financial ruin nevertheless continued to shadow their lives. Once or twice, Winston suggested letting Chartwell, although he quickly dropped the idea when Clementine jumped at it. Clementine knew their future relied on his ability to churn out books and articles at a ferocious rate; they 'lived from book to book, and from one article to the next'. Within the household, their quarrels were the stuff of legend and as she grew older Clementine became increasingly forceful. Her raised voice would sometimes be heard from behind a closed door, only for Winston to emerge afterwards head down and muttering miserably, 'She called me a bloody old fool!'

The only corner of the house immune to Clementine's touch
was her husband's bedroom, a swashbuckling shrine to military
memorabilia with a single bed. Some distance away was
Clementine's far more splendid sky-blue, barrel-domed boudoir,
with its imposing four-poster bed dressed in red moiré silk.
In summer, white roses from the garden graced her desk, and the
windows would be thrown open to capture the fresh air.

Clementine stood by Winston in any number of political meetings over the entirety of their marriage.
Here he was seeking selection as a Liberal candidate in Leicester in 1923 and she was, of course, with him.

•

By the mid-1920s, Winston was convinced that only the Conservatives were capable of countering the Labour Party. Clementine felt duty-bound to follow his re-conversion – at least publicly – taking the spitting, brick-throwing and booing alongside him, but as their daughter, Mary, later related, her mother never made 'a good Tory'.[2] Her feelings about Conservatives, whom she described as variously stupid, inefficient and revelling in 'slaughter & the Army',[3] were doused with suspicion.

Winston nevertheless decisively split with the Liberals over the reunited party's decision to support Labour after the 1923 election. On 29 October 1924, another general election saw the Tories restored to power and secured Winston's return as MP for Epping. His immediate but unexpected appointment in 1928, just before his fiftieth birthday, as Chancellor of the Exchequer effectively completed his homecoming to his old party. Clementine would work tirelessly in his constituency so that Winston could focus on his demanding task at the Treasury. But the fact remained that her husband was now the second most prominent member of a government whose politics were anathema to her. 'The Tories don't want to be made to think!' was one of her private complaints. Certainly they could never provide her with the thrilling pride she had taken during Winston's reforming partnership with Lloyd George. Clementine later told her closest staff that she did not vote Liberal again – out of loyalty to Winston – but she was never to overcome her 'latent, almost subconscious, hostility'[4] to the Tory Party.

No longer sharing her husband's vision, Clementine felt unable to pursue a role of her own on the national stage with any conviction. Despite her efforts to encourage him to help the poor and widows (which he did through modest rises in state pensions), his first Budget in 1925 was widely attacked. Indeed, during his time at the Treasury, Winston had to contend with a period of intense social and industrial strife, much of it arguably of his own making. Yet although Clementine may have felt estranged from her husband's politics, her skill in creating an elegant home with exceptional food made her an asset in his attempts to defuse the various crises that arose. Both sides in the 1925 pre-Budget debate on whether to return to the Gold Standard were bidden to discuss the issue over the Churchill knives and forks, while during the miners' strike of 1926, the Labour opposition leader Ramsay MacDonald sat at the

Clementine fought fifteen elections with Winston and is seen here during the campaign of 1929. She became a doughty performer on the stump in her own right.

Chartwell dining table beside the owners of the coal mines. Flawless hospitality – presided over by Clementine – became part of Winston's surprisingly inclusive political style.[5]

Clementine would welcome numerous British politicians to Chartwell over the years, among them Prime Ministers-to-be Anthony Eden, Harold Macmillan and Edward Heath. She was also to play hostess to some of the world's powerful and famous, including US President Harry Truman, Queen Elizabeth the Queen Mother, Charlie Chaplin and Albert Einstein, the actor Laurence Olivier, Charles de Gaulle and Lawrence of Arabia. Although proud of her aristocratic lineage, Clementine made a point of showing indifference to the very elevated. She was scornful of conspicuous wealth; her daughter, Mary, would even sometimes accuse her of 'inverted snobbishness'. Almost all, however, found Mrs Churchill an alluring hostess. Seated opposite her husband at dinner, visitors were equally surprised when Clementine occasionally admonished him with 'Winston, I wouldn't say that!' or challenged him with 'Winston, you have suddenly changed your mind

When Charlie Chaplin came to visit Chartwell. From left to right: Tom Mitford, Winston, Freddie Birkenhead (partially obscured), Clementine, Diana, Randolph and Charlie Chaplin. 19 September 1932.

Clementine leaving Downing Street to listen to Winston's Budget speech of 1925.

about that!' She was charismatic – and, while there was an air of mystery to her, she had a knack of making guests enjoy the (usually false) impression that they were being paid the honour of being taken into her confidence.

There were times, though, when she would not even attempt to conceal her disapproval of a guest. She took a principled if sectarian stance on many subjects and could erupt at someone spouting the opposing view. She was savage in her putdowns, and the fact that her target was a visitor to her house made scant difference. As a finale, she might storm out of the dining room, leaving her family, including Winston, helpless with embarrassment at what they collectively referred to as one of 'Mama's sweeps'.

•

By the late 1920s, it was clear that regular escapes from Winston were essential to Clementine's health. As she said to Mary, 'it took me all my time and strength just to keep up with [him].'[6] If she ran out of fuel, she would flee. A favourite excuse was taking the 'cure' for fatigue at any number of continental spas, and as life at Chartwell grew ever more exhausting, so her absences grew longer and more frequent. Even when she was in Britain, she spent little time with her children. As Mary noted, although they 'loved and revered her', they did not find in her a 'fun maker or a companion'.

As a result, the Churchill offspring saw little of either parent, even by the standards of British upper-class families of the period. They were not the sort of parents who could be expected to show up at school events and, if on rare occasions their mother did attend, the children were 'ecstatically grateful'. Christmas was the one time of the year when Clementine could bring all her family together with little risk of outside distraction. It was a rare private moment in the family life of a public man and so it *had* to be perfect. Her unstinting pains were also in part compensation for her prolonged absences and what she knew were her shortcomings as a mother. Sarah and Mary drew closer to Clementine as they grew older, but Diana's prickly relationship with her mother would last for the rest of her life. Randolph, meanwhile, was unpopular at school and uncontrollable at home. Clementine's already difficult position as sole disciplinarian of a bumptious and insolent child was aggravated by his habit of running to Winston for an instant reprieve.

Clementine featured on the cover of *The Bystander* magazine in December 1924. Her pared-down style was much admired and copied.

Clementine with her son, Randolph, already by then a difficult teenager,
at Eton on 5 June 1926.

At home with Randolph in 1925.

Lady Blanche had scarcely provided Clementine with a mothering role model. The life of a woman on her own was far from easy in those days, yet she had never made much effort to conceal the fact that Clementine remained too fastidious for her tastes. Then, in March 1925, came news that Clementine's mother, now seventy-seven, was dying and needed her daughter in Dieppe by her side. Clementine loathed the town – not only did she blame its casino for luring her family into penury and her brother, Bill, to an early grave in the cemetery up on the hill, she also felt haunted by Kitty's death from typhoid fever. But, of course, she had to go.

As Clementine nursed her mother through her painful last illness, she did not mention grief in her letters, nor indeed her feelings as to whether Lady Blanche had been a 'true mother'. But, shopping in the Brompton Road in London a few days after her mother's funeral and evidently distracted, she was hit by a bus. She took a taxi home without assistance, but her doctor prescribed her six weeks' rest in Venice to recover. She desperately wanted Winston to make the effort to be with her. Instead he pleaded expense and things to do, claiming, 'Every day away from Chartwell is a day wasted.' It was a sentiment she simply could not share.

Temptation and Redemption

1929–39

As the results flowed into 10 Downing Street on the evening of 30 May 1929, Winston was in a terrifying rage. Once a hope for the future, he was now a disappointment from the past. For the first time, in what became known as the Flapper Election, all women over 21 had been allowed to vote on the same basis as men, the Equal Franchise Act having passed in 1928. Clementine, Diana and Randolph had helped Winston to fight and hold his Epping seat – albeit with a severely reduced majority. But his record as Chancellor was in no small part to blame for the drubbing delivered to Stanley Baldwin's Conservative government. Within days, the Labour Party under Ramsay MacDonald would form its second administration. Winston was to be out of office for a decade – the period frequently referred to as his 'wilderness years'. During this lengthy exile, he would rely on Clementine to comfort him and stand by him no matter what: the effort would test their marriage to breaking point.

Still youthful-looking in her mid-forties outside the Royal Academy, London. Clementine loved looking at art; Winston was more concerned with his own.

Clementine shows her usual support for her husband by accompanying him to the House of Commons on budget day 1929. She was, as always, impeccably dressed for the occasion.

The election result also deprived the Churchills of their London home. Winston and Clementine were reduced once again to living out of suitcases, staying with friends or in hotels. Three years would elapse before their finances were sufficiently robust to allow them to buy another place in the capital. Indeed, when Winston lost £10,000 (over half-a-million pounds in today's money) in the Wall Street crash of 1929, they were on the edge of bankruptcy.

These years marked the beginning of a long period of brittle health for Clementine. In the immediate aftermath of the 1929 defeat, a tonsil infection led to serious blood poisoning and she was sent to a nursing home, where a near-starvation 'curative' regime caused her weight to fall to eight stone six. The illness was followed by bouts of mastoid disease, a potentially fatal infection of the air cells behind the ear. So severe was the pain at one point that her doctors were forced to operate twice in a day. But as usual in a real crisis, Clementine rose to the challenge and astonished them with her courage.

The drama drew the best out of Winston as well: he took the trouble to sit by her bedside, patiently reading her psalms. He was less attentive, though, during her increasingly frequent bouts of non-specific nervous exhaustion. Despite his own much-hyped Black Dog, in truth he had no understanding of real depression, whereas at times Clementine's was acute. Few on the outside would guess, but she would spend the rest of her life trying increasingly invasive and unorthodox methods of overcoming it.

As well as politics, painting and writing, Winston devoted much time during these years to his 'cronies'. Clementine disapproved of hangers-on like the unmarried Irish loner Brendan Bracken and the hard-drinking F.E. Smith (Lord Birkenhead), perhaps Winston's closest friend, likening them to 'dogs round a lamp-post'.[1] But she was most horrified by the hold that Canadian Lord Beaverbrook, a rapacious wheeler-dealer of uncertain loyalties and a shady past, seemed to have over Winston. The newspaper magnate played manipulative power games, and Clementine almost always (and often correctly) vehemently disagreed with his political advice to her husband.

In 1932, during a trip to Bavaria, Winston was struck by displays of what he considered to be the distinctly unhealthy militarism of the National Socialists. From then on 'Germany's card was marked'[2] in his mind and he became deeply troubled about the potential Nazi threat. Just how much Clementine shared his obsession with the Nazi peril in those early days is not clear, although she made sure to keep abreast of the news, and cut out articles on events in Germany for Winston that she thought might be of use. When she was away, he wrote to her frequently of his concerns, but in the early 1930s, she rarely addressed the subject directly in her replies.

Whatever the level of agreement on the German issue, in most other areas their marriage was turbulent. They were profoundly at odds over how to deal with what was now widely viewed as Randolph's 'pathological' self-importance. Clementine rarely put pen to paper regarding her son at this time, but Mary recalled bitter rows and recriminations between her parents on the subject and a distinct chilliness in their relations. Although Winston would rebuke Randolph when he was rude to his mother, and send him from the room when he refused to apologise, his inclination was still to relent. John Julius Norwich, a Churchill family friend, believed that she really did 'hate' her son, and that he in turn held her in equally low regard.[3]

The tragedy was that on the odd occasion they did spend time together away from Winston and Chartwell, Clementine and Randolph enjoyed each other's company. In October 1930, when he was just nineteen, Randolph dropped his studies at Oxford to take up an invitation to give a lecture tour in the US. Word soon came back that he had met a young woman and was planning to marry her. Clementine hurriedly set out for New York in February 1931 to try to persuade him that he was too young to settle down. Upon reaching her son, she was surprised by his reception of her and sat talking with him long into the night. Away from the pressures of being Winston Churchill's heir, she saw her son in a new light. Randolph 'is a darling. He has quite captivated me … It is quite like a honeymoon.'[4]

Previously, both Clementine and Winston had been known to be 'hostile' to America as a result of President Coolidge's crushing announcement in

●

Whatever the level of agreement on the German issue,
in most other areas their marriage was turbulent. They were
profoundly at odds over how to deal with what was now
widely viewed as Randolph's 'pathological' self-importance.

●

Clementine and Diana accompany Winston on his 1931 lecture tour of the US, travelling in style on the S.S. *Bremen*. Despite appearances, they were virtually bankrupt and desperately needed the money.

1928 that he would not forgive Britain's crippling debts from the Great War. Clementine had been hawkish, too, in her attitude to American ambitions to supplant Britain as a world power. Now she had mingled with such enjoyment in American society, her whole conception of the Land of the Free was dramatically altered.

Sadly, when she and Randolph returned to Winston and life in England after this harmonious interlude, their relationship plummeted to new depths of distrust. To Clementine's horror, in 1934, Winston was obliged to settle pressing gambling debts of £1,500, wiping out a tenth of his entire earnings for the year in one go. Sometimes Winston refused to see Randolph; more than once Clementine banned him from the house completely. Relations deteriorated to the point where Clementine, although never intimidated by her husband, began to fear her son.

The early 1930s also highlighted the Churchills' parental shortcomings in preparing their elder daughters for adulthood. In truth, having received so little parenting themselves, Clementine and Winston were struggling to find their way. Diana had made her society debut in 1927, during the same season as her second cousin, the stunningly beautiful Diana Mitford. It was, of course, the latter who had taken London by storm, and both Diana Churchill and her parents had found the contrast with her namesake humiliating. Perhaps Clementine had forgotten her own pain at being eclipsed by her vivacious sister, Kitty, for she took little care to hide her disappointment from her daughter. Diana sought consolation by pursuing a career on the stage but found she had little real talent.

Salvation appeared to arrive in 1932, in the form of a proposal from handsome John Bailey, the son of a South African mine-owner. The wedding, held on 12 December at St Margaret's, Westminster, was suitably grand; the trouble was that Bailey was in love with the romantic novelist and society beauty Barbara Cartland, who on discovering his 'impossible' drinking had sensibly run a mile. Diana discovered her mistake much too late; the marriage broke down after just a year.

Sarah's future was also uncertain. Upon coming out in 1933, she found the round of society balls excruciating. She wanted to follow her sister, Diana, into acting. Despite her own thwarted ambition to go to university, Clementine could summon no empathy for either daughter's theatrical dreams, dismissing both girls as without 'talent or even aptitude'.[5] Only Mary seemed to be growing up largely trouble-free.

Now she had mingled with such enjoyment in American society, her whole conception of the Land of the Free was dramatically altered.

Clementine and Winston
take their daughter Sarah
to be presented at court
in May 1933.

In December 1934, the wealthy Guinness heir Lord Moyne, one of Winston's
former junior ministers at the Treasury, invited the Churchills on a four-
month cruise to the East Indies. Too busy with politics and book writing,
Winston decided not to take up the offer, but Clementine was determined
to go. It was while sailing across the glittering seas on board Moyne's
sumptuous motor yacht, *Rosaura*, that she was thrown into the company
of Terence Philip. Tall, rich, suave, an authority on art and unburdened by
driving ambition – in fact, unlike Winston in almost every respect – he was
also an entertaining gossip, seven years her junior and complimented her

lavishly on her beauty and brains, while seeking little in return. On board the *Rosaura*, sunshine and champagne soon swept her up onto a thrilling high. The gloom of European politics, Winston's obsession with his faltering career, her children's troubles – all rapidly retreated over the horizon. After years of isolation and anxiety, she had at last found companionship, as well as a release of tension. Excited by the attentions of such a man, she fell in love. Their sunlit holiday fling may have been almost entirely innocent and was in any case eventually to fizzle out under the grey skies of England. But it restored her strength and energy, and when she finally returned to Winston – and real life – on 30 April 1935, Clementine was a revitalised woman with a model's physique.

In 1935, Winston spent Christmas away from his family in Morocco, so Clementine seized the opportunity to spend more time alone with Mary. Their skiing trip to Zürs in Austria, which Mary remembered as a 'great

Clementine and Winston escort Mary to Westminster Hall in 1935 for a ceremony in which the then king and queen were to receive an address of congratulations from both houses of Parliament.

The celebrated photographer Madame Yevonde took this picture for *Tatler* in December 1933. Clementine was already forty-eight, but some thought her more beautiful than ever.

thrill', was their first proper holiday together. Clementine became a stylish if not especially speedy skier, but at least she now shared a hobby with Mary, and she made plenty of time for them to chat and read together in the evening. Only now did Mary come to know and understand her hitherto distant mother as a 'person'. The experiment was such a success that it was repeated the following winter, and the next; the trips established a companionship between them that would rarely falter.

While Clementine was away, Sarah informed her father that she was in love with comedian Vic Oliver. Although he was eighteen years older, divorced and with a devoted mistress in New York, Sarah had set her heart on becoming his wife. In the absence of Clementine's wiser counsel, Winston reacted with fury. But her father's aggression made Sarah all the more determined. After she promised not to marry Oliver, Winston claimed triumphantly to Diana: 'I think I have put her off.' 'On the contrary,' replied the perceptive Diana. 'I think you have chased her away.'[6]

Sensing imminent disaster, Clementine finally returned from her holiday to try a less confrontational approach. Over breakfast at Chartwell, she promised Sarah her own flat in London to use with 'total freedom', on the condition that she gave up Oliver. An offer that would have been unthinkable just a few months earlier, it not only showed how Clementine's attitudes had relaxed since her adventures aboard the *Rosaura*, but also revealed how desperate she was not to lose her daughter. Shocked at what she saw as her mother's 'immoral' suggestion, Sarah was not in any case tempted by the parade of eligible young bachelors her mother hastily invited to Chartwell. She appreciated her mother's conciliatory efforts, but her mind was made up.

In September 1936, with Winston safely out of the country in the south of France, Sarah bolted for New York, imploring Clementine in a letter to 'Please make Papa understand'. Clementine was distraught, and certain that Winston would not be mollified. Randolph was dispatched on the next steamer across the Atlantic, lawyers were instructed to erect legal barriers and private detectives were hired to dig up dirt on Oliver. Regardless, the couple were quickly and quietly married on Christmas Eve 1936.

Clementine's judgement during the abdication crisis of 1936 was more astute. She and Winston fought bitterly over whether the new King, Edward VIII (George V having died in January), should be forced to renounce the throne if he were to marry his twice-divorced American mistress, Wallis Simpson. Prime Minister Stanley Baldwin had bluntly informed the King

•

It was while sailing across the glittering seas on board Moyne's sumptuous motor yacht, *Rosaura*, that she was thrown into the company of Terence Philip.

•

Opposite: Unlike Winston, who preferred more sedentary pursuits, Clementine enjoyed the sport and socialising at tennis parties and played on until late middle-age. Here she is attending a gathering held by Lady Crosfield in Highgate, north London, in 1933.

that Mrs Simpson would be unacceptable as Queen, and that he would have to choose between her and his crown. Despite Clementine's warning, Winston rose to speak in Edward's defence in the House of Commons in December 1936, and was immediately 'howled down' in shame. By ignoring her advice, he had made a near career-ending misjudgement of the mood of the House.

The incident had shaken even Clementine's faith that Winston would one day reach Number 10, when for so long she had believed his destiny was surely to take the top job. She had endured so much but his latest humiliations took her close to breaking point. Exhausted, depressed, without hope for the future, she started planning her way out. She went to see sister-in-law, Goonie, to say that she wanted a divorce.[7] Goonie wisely advised her to go abroad to reflect before she finally made up her mind.

It was only when Clementine duly left for Austria that Winston appears to have realised that he might lose his wife as well as his daughter. When Sarah returned to Britain, he invited her to a reconciliation lunch at Chartwell. Few were surprised when the relationship with Oliver quickly began to unravel. Its demise left Sarah deeply unhappy and, by the end of the decade she, like Randolph and Diana, was drinking heavily. But at least Winston's efforts to broker a peace with his daughter won him favour with his wife, who returned from Austria a little pacified.

•

Despite the growing military threat from both Germany and Italy, in November 1935, the Conservatives had won the election on the pledge that there would be 'no great armaments'. Unsurprisingly, therefore, the most 'belligerent' exponent of rapid rearmament had again been excluded from the new government. But Clementine now saw that Winston's continued exile might leave him untainted by the government's continuing blunders. From this point on, Winston changed his tactics, seeking to broaden his appeal and win support from a wider spectrum of public opinion.

His attempt to build an anti-Nazi coalition led Clementine to take a closer interest in Winston's campaign. Events in Europe were in any case gathering pace. In March 1936, Hitler defied the Treaty of Versailles by reoccupying the

•

Winston remained obstinately outspoken as the decade wore on, even though most people were 'keener on hearing what Hitler said about peace than what Churchill said about war'.

•

demilitarised zone of the Rhineland. Then in July, nationalist elements of the Spanish army revolted against the Republican government and a bloody civil war broke out. The Soviets moved to prop up the Republic while Hitler and Mussolini began supplying military aid to General Franco's rebels. Having initially hoped that the Communists would be 'crushed', Winston now began to fear that a nationalist victory in Madrid would result in Spain falling under the influence of Nazi Germany. By the late 1930s, the Spanish Civil War was to prove a turning point for public opinion in Britain, demonstrating that bloodshed was the only way to halt the spread of fascism.

Groups of unlikely allies haunted by the idea that Britain could eventually suffer the fate of Spain began converging on Chartwell to stop the madness of appeasement. Clementine's home was now the venue for covert meetings between military officers, civil servants, journalists and industrialists, as well as refugee Germans, Czechs and Austrians. Once again, Clementine found herself welcoming and hosting – often in great secrecy – powerful and influential visitors. Drawn into the frantic activity, she became universally trusted for her tact and discretion. She also helped to establish a network of informants on Germany's massive rearmament, recruiting one of her own cousins who fed details back from Prague.

In May 1937, Baldwin retired as Prime Minister to be replaced by Neville Chamberlain, under whose leadership the division between supporters of appeasement, like himself, and critics such as Winston became even more personal and bitter. Every moment of the Churchill day was now feverishly devoted to proving to a disbelieving nation the horrifying scale of the Nazi threat. His staff worked all hours, one even suffering a stroke from overwork. Clementine, too, sometimes felt overwhelmed, once exclaiming to her nephew, Johnny, 'I can't stand it any longer',[8] but she was nevertheless just as devoted to the cause as her husband.

Winston remained obstinately outspoken as the decade wore on, even though most people were 'keener on hearing what Hitler said about peace than what Churchill said about war'.[9] After the *Anschluss*, with Austria incorporated into a Greater German Reich, he was nevertheless able to warn that Czechoslovakia would be next. Indeed, Hitler was demanding control of those parts of the country with large German populations, stoking fears that war was inevitable. The British Fleet was mobilised and air-raid trenches were dug in London's parks. When, on 29 September 1938, Neville Chamberlain went to meet Hitler and Mussolini, he was comprehensively duped,

Winston delivers a speech warning against disarmament at the Conservative Party conference in Bournemouth in 1935. Clementine, seen in the background, was one of his few followers during this fallow period of his career.

sacrificing Czechoslovakia to Hitler's demands in a naive belief that by doing so he could avert war. The Churchills and their growing band of supporters saw his capitulation as a final act of foolish betrayal.

Exhausted by tension and emotion, Clementine, now fifty-three, was also nursing a painful broken toe. An invitation from Lord Moyne to cruise to the Caribbean therefore seemed too good to refuse – even without Terence Philip, and despite the mounting international crisis. Yet, although the *Rosaura* was the same beautiful boat, little else resembled Clementine's previous voyage. Lord Moyne was chairing a Royal Commission into social conditions in the West Indies and the purpose of the trip was investigation, not adventure or relaxation. As a result, Clementine witnessed the terrible deprivation of the British Empire's Caribbean holdings. Not only did it horrify her, it provoked her to give vent to her anger at what she saw as Tory complacency, and she admitted finding much in common with the Labour members of the Royal Commission who travelled with her. It was her sense of injustice – and her political creed – rather than her longing for romance that was reawakened on this trip.

Below: Clementine accompanies Winston to an election meeting in his Epping constituency in 1929. She attended far more meetings and got far more involved than other political wives.

Clementine and her daughter, Diana, attend the first night of *Follow the Sun* at the Adelphi Theatre, London, in February 1936. Sarah Churchill was one of the dancers.

In Jamaica, she told Winston that she was 'thrilled' when raucously cheered as the 'wife of the future prime minister of England',[10] the crowd hailing him as an anti-fascist scourge and even a saviour. He duly sent her detailed typed political bulletins marked 'secret' on the growing fears for France and the Chamberlain government's woeful unpreparedness for war. She, in turn, became increasingly uneasy about how isolated Winston must be feeling in her absence. When, after listening to a radio broadcast from England on 24 January 1939, Moyne's mistress, Vera Broughton, led attacks on her embattled husband for endangering Chamberlain's so-called peace, it was like a call to arms. A revivified Clementine flounced out majestically, booking her passage on the first steamer home.

Just six weeks later, on 15 March, Hitler's troops invaded the rump of Czechoslovakia, followed soon after on Good Friday by Mussolini's annexation of Albania. Now, at last, much of the press – even his old enemies at the *Daily Mail* – began to row in behind Winston. Her doubts and anxieties put to one side, Clementine was back on form and soon giving rousing speeches in his constituency – denouncing Hitler, calling for national unity and fearlessly blaming Chamberlain's government for the crisis engulfing Europe. 'At any rate,' she informed a sizeable crowd in Chigwell in July, 'we have made up our minds to do our duty, whatever may befall!'[11]

World of Accident and Storm

1939–40

Clementine sat bolt upright in the Distinguished Strangers'
Gallery, eyes fixed on her husband in the Commons' chamber
below. For years the House had mocked Winston and his
warnings about the Nazi threat. Now his predictions had
come true and she saw how it was finally uniting with him in
a 'temper for war'. At dawn that morning – 1 September 1939
– Germany had brutally attacked Poland. With the news
growing worse by the hour, Neville Chamberlain had finally
admitted to Parliament that the time had come 'when action
rather than speech is required'.

Clementine became the human face of the Churchill
government during the war. She took a leaf out of
Eleanor Roosevelt's book and made sure she joined
in with factory workers on her frequent morale-
boosting visits. They loved her for it.

The following day, Clementine was in the House again. Britain had at last mobilised its forces; children were being evacuated from London and anxious crowds were gathering in the streets. Seven hundred miles to the east, the Wehrmacht was smashing the valiant but ill-equipped Polish army and laying waste towns and villages. Britain was honour-bound by treaty to defend Poland. Yet still Chamberlain failed to make the move.

At 10.30 p.m. Winston and Clementine played host to a stream of grave-faced Members of Parliament, all in a state of 'bewildered rage'. Duff Cooper noticed how Clementine was 'more violent in her denunciation of the Prime Minister even than Winston'.[1] Chamberlain had led them all to believe he *was* finally going to take a stand against Hitler, but still no word had come and it was now clear that he was once more backtracking on his pledge. As rain pummelled the windows and thunder crashed round the Westminster rooftops, the assembled men begged Winston to take a lead. At last he sat down to write, bluntly warning Chamberlain of the 'injury' done to the 'spirit of national unity by the apparent weakening of our resolve'.

Finally, at daybreak, the Prime Minister issued an ultimatum to Germany to halt its hostilities against Poland. As he famously broadcast soon afterwards, 'no such undertaking' was received and, on 3 September 1939, Britain declared war on Germany. After listening to Chamberlain on the radio, Clementine joined Winston on their roof terrace. They watched the first barrage balloons rising slowly over the roofs and spires of London, and thought of the horrors to come. Yet they were far from downcast and Winston noted how Clementine was equally 'braced' for whatever the future held.

Later that day, the Prime Minister summoned Winston to Downing Street and, while Clementine waited in the car outside, appointed Winston First Lord of the Admiralty. In an early indication of how they would work during the years ahead, she accompanied her husband as he immediately set about a tour of naval bases. Back in London, she began to gather Winston's supporters. The day after he took office, she arranged a lunch for twenty-four. So began a life with 'less schedule than a forest fire and less peace than a hurricane', in the words of their bodyguard, Walter Thompson.[2] For the second time, Clementine was at Winston's side as he galvanised the Admiralty for war.

Britain's early naval engagements, however, failed to go his way. Clementine wrote to her sister, Nellie, on 20 September 1939, that the news was 'grim beyond words'.[3] The sinking, on 14 October 1939, of the HMS *Royal Oak*, while anchored at Scapa Flow in the Orkney Islands, cost 833 lives. Within a month, 60,000 tons of British shipping had been destroyed by magnetic mines alone. Yet many now believed that Winston's fanatical drive made him the only politician capable of leading Britain to victory.

Meanwhile, Clementine masterminded the couple's move into Winston's beloved Admiralty House. Under her orders, the First Lord's office was transformed into a modern command centre. She arranged his desk at an angle so that he would not be distracted by views of the park, and made sure his chair was practical and uncushioned; but she also had two armchairs, upholstered in comforting red leather, positioned beside the coal-burning fire, and placed a constantly replenished biscuit tin and soda siphon for his whiskies on a nearby table. She did everything she could to ease her husband's burden – he was not to be bothered by any domestic care. Winston's day was long and arduous, but he made a point of joining Clementine – and their guests – for both lunch and dinner. He also kept her constantly informed. If news came in of a battle, he would often rush to tell her. She joined him on the quayside at Plymouth when victorious ships sailed in; she would also accompany him to speak to the relatives of those who had lost their lives. It was her idea, when the crews from the battle of the River Plate were being honoured, to set up a special enclosure on Horse Guards Parade for the families of the bereaved in order to show them respect and consideration. And, more than twenty years since she had last launched a ship, she was invited back to do the honours for the aircraft carrier *Indomitable*.

She threw herself into all aspects of the war effort and it visibly thrilled her. Clementine was 'more beautiful now than in early life', and was as 'fearless and indefatigable' as her husband, noted Lady Diana Cooper in March 1940.[4] The way she helped to run Fulmer Chase maternity hospital for officers' wives in Buckinghamshire (where she made a point of visiting almost every expectant mother herself) was deemed 'beyond praise' by a midwifery magazine.

Conscious of the need to set an example to the nation, Clementine expected *all* the family to do their duty. Mary, just out of school, worked in a canteen and for the Red Cross; later, she would receive her mother's encouragement when she decided to join the Auxiliary Territorial Service (ATS) in one of its new 'mixed' anti-aircraft batteries. Sarah joined the

•

She threw herself into all aspects of the war effort and it visibly thrilled her. Clementine was 'more beautiful now than in early life', and was as 'fearless and indefatigable' as her husband, noted Lady Diana Cooper in March 1940.

•

Clementine made a point of welcoming any support in the war from the US, even before it joined the fighting after Pearl Harbor. Her charm and charisma won her many devoted fans and here she is seen at a party for American nurses who had crossed the Atlantic to help out.

Clementine was proud of her service-girl daughters, Mary (left) and Sarah (right), believing that women from all backgrounds should do their bit for the war. 18 January 1944.

Women's Auxiliary Air Force (WAAF) and was assigned to the Photographic Interpretation Unit at RAF Medmenham. Only Diana struggled to find a significant role: she became an officer with the Women's Royal Navy Service (WRNS) but resigned her commission for 'family reasons' (although later she became an air-raid warden).

Meanwhile, when Randolph – with his regiment, the 4th Hussars, about to be posted abroad – asked Pamela, eldest daughter of Lord and Lady Digby, for her hand in marriage, the wedding was hastily arranged for 4 October at St John's church, Smith Square. As Clementine had feared, it was not to be a happy union. Pamela did her conjugal duty by quickly becoming pregnant; he failed miserably in his. He lost money they did not have by gambling with rich friends, drank more than ever and was frequently abusive. Yet Pamela's disillusion with her husband created a natural intimacy with his mother. Drawing on her own handling of Winston, Clementine counselled Pamela on how to deal with Randolph: 'Darling, go away. Don't say where you're going. Just disappear. I...would go off to a hotel for three days and he wouldn't hear from me.'[5]

•

The first eight months of the war were eerily quiet. The initially buoyant mood had given way by the end of 1939, when the expected 'rain of bombs' failed to pour, to bewildered resentment. The enemy was yet to kill more than three soldiers, but the blackout imposed in Britain had already taken 4,000 lives in accidents.[6] Moreover, millions had been uprooted from the cities to a countryside they often loathed. Essentials from soap to sugar soon soared in price. Only the rich appeared conspicuously free of hardship.

Chamberlain's wartime Downing Street merely exacerbated these feelings of division and inertia, senior officials remaining convinced that real fighting could be avoided. Clementine was merciless in her criticism of Chamberlain's complacency. Shored up by a large Conservative majority in the Commons, it recalled to her the lassitude of the Asquith administration early in the previous war.

The so-called 'phoney war', however, came to an abrupt end in the spring of 1940. The Germans invaded Norway, who appealed to Britain for help.

•

Clementine's prediction had finally come true: at the age of sixty-five, Winston had been called on to serve the nation as its leader. Their true life's work together could now begin.

•

When the ensuing naval and military expedition was badly bungled, Clementine worried that the Norwegian fiasco would bring Winston down in the same fashion as had the Dardanelles.

On 7 May 1940, attention once again turned to the Commons, and a dramatic debate on whether the government was still fit to conduct the war. Although the government won the subsequent vote, it was clear that Chamberlain's Tory administration was fatally damaged. Chamberlain would have to go – providing Winston with his chance at last.

At this critical time, Clementine received news that Nellie was in desperate need of her at her home in Herefordshire. Nellie's husband, Bertram, had died on 6 May and her son, Giles, a *Daily Express* reporter, had been captured in Norway and taken prisoner by the Germans. Although desperately torn, she decided on 8 May she must go.

Two days later, the German army launched a 'lightning-fast' offensive through Western Europe towards the Channel. With an invasion of Britain surely just days away, Chamberlain summoned Winston and Foreign Secretary Lord Halifax to Downing Street to announce his reluctant decision to stand down. As Winston later wrote, it quickly became clear that the 'duty' of saving his country had 'fallen' on him. He immediately phoned Clementine to tell her the news and she boarded the first train back to London; she was waiting excitedly for him in the drawing room, still wearing her hat, when he dashed back to their quarters in Admiralty House. Clementine's prediction had finally come true: at the age of sixty-five, Winston had been called on to serve the nation as its leader. Their true life's work together could now begin.

While the country faced the imminent peril of a Nazi invasion, however, Clementine became aware of dangers closer to home. As one close observer put it, Winston was becoming 'virtually a dictator'.[7] He terrified ministers, military commanders and officials by his sheer force of will; even by his family's account, his leadership style was 'tyrannical'. When Clementine learned from an unnamed 'devoted friend' that Winston risked, if not outright 'rebellion' from his staff, then a hostile 'slave mentality', she took to paper. 'I hope you will forgive me if I tell you something that I feel you ought to know,' her letter began. There was a 'danger' of him being 'disliked' because of his increasingly 'rough, sarcastic and overbearing manner'. 'It is for you to give the orders and if they are bungled – except for the King, the Archbishop of Canterbury and the Speaker you can sack anyone and everyone,' she advised.

Randolph (centre) was Clementine's only son but her relationship with him was strained for most of his life. Here the Churchills celebrate his 1939 marriage to Pamela Digby, but the union was not to last and she went on to become the 'twentieth century's most influential courtesan'.

'Therefore with this terrific power you must combine urbanity, kindness and if possible Olympic calm.'

Having observed Winston's mistakes during the Great War, Clementine well understood the hazards of his tendency to browbeat opposition. She had warned him since before the Dardanelles disaster that a culture of passive acquiescence was potentially dangerous, and now she took it on herself to act as a corrective. One by one key staff were invited to take tea with her, alone – first at the Admiralty flat, and later in the elegant White Drawing Room at Downing Street (which she made her private retreat). Here she made them feel appreciated; giving them her undivided attention, but all the while sounding them out for signs of trouble.

No answer to her letter exists, but there is no doubt that Winston changed as a result. While his staff continued to find him on occasion impossible, his 'ill-tempered phase', recalled his private secretary, Jock Colville, was a 'passing one'.[8] He quickly learned the conciliatory power of small gestures, once laying his hand on the shoulder of another private secretary and saying, 'I may seem very fierce, but I am fierce only with one man – Hitler.'[9] Living above the shop in Downing Street, Clementine thereafter closely monitored his behaviour. As daughter-in-law Pamela noted, her intervention demonstrated to others 'that she was an enormously important component in the whole thing...and a very important balance for him'.[10]

Clementine chose her moments to intervene carefully. During intense discussions with military chiefs, for instance, Winston would sometimes become 'difficult' and start stomping round the room, at which point she might say: 'Now, Winston, that's all right, the subject can be let rest for the moment. We are going to have luncheon.' General Sir Frederick Pile, chief of Anti-Aircraft Command, witnessed her mediation skills on many such an occasion and recalled that 'she bossed him – but in the most delightful way – with great affection and with the deepest understanding of his nature'.[11]

•

June 1940 was a critical moment of the war. France was on the point of capitulation, and German troops were already marching through Paris. Faced with Winston's stubborn refusal to avoid taking risks, his officials found

Opposite: Clementine had a famous knack for lending her surroundings glamour. During and after the war Downing Street became shabby and down-at-heel but was transformed by her magic touch and invitations were highly sought after.

•

She took pains to set an example. From July 1941, she would take on the hazardous work of a fire watcher: perched on a prominent rooftop during air raids, surrounded by the deafening clatter of gunfire and choking on the stench of sulphur and gunpowder

•

themselves desperate for an alternative authority to appeal to if difficult decisions were to be made. When he resolved to fly to France through a rare spell of rough weather to try to convince its leaders to continue fighting, the Air Staff – having exhausted other avenues in their effort to persuade him it was too dangerous – petitioned Clementine. She listened and then asked: 'Are the Air Force flying today?' They answered: 'Yes, of course – on operations.' She replied, 'Well, isn't Winston going on an operation?' Her decision, as it so often would be in future, was final.

Despite her evident skills, however, it took Clementine longer than Winston to gain acceptance, let alone affection, in government circles. In 1940, Downing Street – like the rest of Whitehall – was run almost entirely by public-school-educated men with a certain narrow world view. Few took kindly to the fact that Clementine was no ordinary, biddable political wife. Despite lacking the mandate of the ballot box, she was often both opinionated and forceful; she saw it as her duty to help Winston win the war in any way she could.

Clementine moreover recognised from the beginning that this was to be a war fought by men, but that victory would depend on the endurance and strength of women. She, like many others, had discovered what she was capable of when called to action in the First World War, only to retreat back into the domestic bubble. Now, with Britain facing an even greater crisis, women were to be more vital than ever.

She took pains to set an example. From July 1941, she would take on the hazardous work of a fire watcher: perched on a prominent rooftop during air raids, surrounded by the deafening clatter of gunfire and choking on the stench of sulphur and gunpowder, she braved the attendant dangers of being badly burned, cut by shrapnel or worse.

Clementine was also intimately involved in the overall direction of the war. She frequently accompanied Winston on visits to garrisons, seaside town defences and, during the Battle of Britain, the RAF fighter command centre at Uxbridge. On the cloudless day of 15 September 1940, she descended with him to the dark of the Operations Room, where she watched the direction of what would prove to be the decisive confrontation in British skies.

Frequently seen smiling alongside her husband, Clementine became the human face of Winston's government and made sure her well-groomed and stylish appearance (in the midst of the Blitz) expressed a confidence in victory at all times. In the absence of hot water due to bomb damage in

Clementine with Winston (wearing air commodore uniform) leaving 10 Downing
Street in February 1940, three months before he became Prime Minister.

Clementine cheerfully dons a Polish officer's great coat to ward off the cold on an inspection of Polish troops in St Andrews, Scotland. She was well aware of the powerful symbolism of such gestures when both nations were fighting against the Nazis.

•

On the cloudless day of 15 September 1940,
she descended with him to the dark of the
Operations Room, where she watched the direction
of what would prove to be the decisive
confrontation in British skies.

•

Downing Street, she washed her hair, to her family's alarm, with neat
benzene to give it shine. Her wardrobe was also carefully chosen to send out
subliminal messages of defiance through strong colours – one favourite was
a coral red – and bold eye-catching styles. Like the Queen, she continued to
believe she should dress up to meet the people, just as they would do for her,
and that a touch of glamour was welcome amid the shabbiness of war.

Her growing popular appeal was recognised by the Ministry of
Information, which in September commissioned the society photographer
Cecil Beaton to take pictures of her at Downing Street. As he waited for her,
Beaton inspected the 'delightful' reception rooms, where the sun streamed
in on bowls of sweet peas from Chartwell and the pale-coloured walls were
covered with Sickert sketches, Nicholson still-lifes and family photographs.
Then Clementine, whom he described as 'a bright, unspoilt and girlish
woman', appeared and sat on the sofa, elegantly pouring tea in evening
dress with her hair glamorously set like 'Pallas Athene', the Greek goddess
of courage.

The photographs duly appeared in *Picture Post* in November 1940. Her
mailbag ballooned, and through the correspondence she developed a keen
feel for popular opinion – information that fed directly into Winston's
speech-making, public persona and government policy. As Winston's doctor,
Lord Moran, put it in his diaries: 'His countrymen have come to feel that
he is saying what they would like to say for themselves if they knew how.'[12]

Clementine knew that Winston lived his life in 'blinkers', and by
temperament and background was oblivious to the mindset of the great
majority. But there could be no repeat of the loftiness displayed by Asquith in
the last war. The collective spirit of 'we can take it' – which was almost all that
Britain had going for it in 1940 – had to be kept alive. So, with the help of
her loyal secretary, Grace Hamblin, Clementine answered as many letters as

Clementine looks as if she has just given Winston the benefit of her views on something. They are travelling down the Thames together to visit east London after a bad bombing raid blocked the roads. 25 September 1940.

possible personally and championed countless causes. Many concerned the discomforts and distress caused by the war at home, such as the woeful condition of air-raid shelters in London when the Blitz started in September 1940. Heaters, full-sized beds, well-lit and clean latrines, disinfected bedding, extra shelters and a host of other improvements were provided as a direct result of her specific interventions, earning the gratitude of the beneficiaries. Marjorie K. Hopkins of 191 Commercial Road, east London, wrote to her on 6 July 1941: 'I find it very difficult to thank you adequately for coming to see us at Stepney last Wednesday… I cannot tell you how much it cheered us up to be able to tell you myself some of my most urgent problems…I feel now at last thanks to you something will be done.' Often Clementine would simply write to the relevant minister, but on other occasions she would dragoon such an individual into chaperoning her on an unannounced inspection. It was an 'invitation' that even members of the Cabinet felt unable to decline. She even recruited her long-term adversary Lord Beaverbrook (then Minister of Supply) to deal with a crisis in the supply of beds, knowing that his talents were perfectly suited to solving a 'blockage'. Sure enough, within weeks, two million new beds were being manufactured.

With a Red Cross representative and, more often than not, Jock Colville in tow, she could inspect five different establishments in different parts of London within the space of three hours, leaving others gasping in her wake. What made her so effective was not only her practical approach – honed in the canteens of the previous world war – but also how judiciously she used her position. Understanding the importance of symbols, she almost always wore a turban to pay tribute to the female munitions workers who were obliged to put one on to keep their hair away from machinery or chemicals. Clementine's were admittedly made from fine silks or chiffons, printed with extracts from Winston's speeches, but her solidarity was clear.

For all her various contributions to the war effort, Clementine remained rigidly focused on Winston; she was, quite literally, always there for him. His staff kept her informed of when his meetings were likely to finish so that she could return home shortly beforehand, and she was almost unfailingly present at mealtimes. Often he assumed she had been waiting for him all day.

•

The Churchills were almost always seen together on their frequent tours of bombsites during the Blitz. Here they are touring streets in the City of London in 1940 after a raid.

After the RAF's victory in the Battle of Britain, the immediate threat of invasion receded, but the Blitz that followed killed 44,000 civilians and rendered the centres of the target cities almost unrecognisable. Clementine displayed characteristic resolve during the raids, sometimes calmly finishing her cup of tea in the Downing Street garden even while the warning sirens wailed beyond.

Number 10 was, of course, an obvious target and in October a bomb narrowly missed the building, killing four people nearby. Mercifully, the residence did not catch fire, but the Churchills were left without gas or hot water. Afterwards, they moved their beds from Downing Street into the Annexe, a flat created from the more solidly built government offices round the corner at Storey's Gate, protected by thick metal shutters at the windows and located directly above the heavily reinforced Central War Rooms. Inside, Clementine had the walls painted pastel colours and enlivened the décor with soft lighting, good furniture, a George Romney painting over the fireplace and a George Frederic Watts portrait of a young Lady Blanche. Next door, with the help of chintz hangings, she had softened another office space into her bedroom. Within these peaceful rooms, the war seemed far away.

The Blitz required Clementine to restrain Winston's more reckless instincts. His highly dangerous excursions into the London streets during air raids – drawn by the people's cheery resilience – provoked alarm among his officials, and they approached Clementine to help. The next time he had the urge to go out during the bombing, she was ready in coat and scarf to join him. This time, concerned for *her* safety, he avoided the worst of the raid. 'This was her technique,' recalled Pug Ismay. 'She knew precisely how to handle him.' Her presence also made his impromptu visits all the more popular. Women were particularly cheered by her arrival and would surge forward to greet her. Despite her normal rigid self-control in public, Clementine was sometimes overcome. On one bombsite visit, with eyes welling up, she was heard to murmur: 'Pray God, we don't let them down.'[13]

> With Winston's reputation more important than ever, Clementine lived in fear that her eldest children, particularly her son, might dishonour it.

With Winston's reputation more important than ever, Clementine lived in fear that her eldest children, particularly her son, might dishonour it. Pamela and Randolph's only child together, little Winston, was born in his grandfather's bedroom at Chequers at 4.40 a.m. on 10 October 1940, not long after a large bomb had exploded nearby. Despite intrusive security, Clementine and the family were never safe at Chequers; positioned close to high ground, it was vulnerable to aerial attack, particularly on moonlit nights. An alternative weekend retreat was needed and Ditchley Park in Oxfordshire, owned by the Anglo-American Conservative MP Ronald Tree, was selected. Bigger, smarter and better heated than Chequers – and discreetly located down a long single-track road – Ditchley was a bona fide stately home.

Here, as at Chequers and Downing Street, Clementine's hospitality knew no bounds; she believed it did much to bind people together and give them strength to go on through the interminable pressures of war. Guests were greeted in the fifty-foot-long library, with its two marble fireplaces, red leather sofas and towering bookcases, and ate in the opulent dining room beneath a huge chandelier and twinkling sconces. Having insisted that the Churchills were issued with the same ration cards as everyone else, Clementine was well aware how challenging it was to produce good food on coupons. Fortunately, the meagre fare available was regularly topped up by friends and well-wishers, either from their own farms or from abroad, as well as from the extra supplies permitted for government entertaining. But even in her privileged position, it was a struggle to cater for Winston's high expectations, not least because he liked to conduct much of his business over the dining table. Mercifully for all, Clementine hired Georgina Landemare, who had previously helped out occasionally at Chartwell, to work for her full time at Downing Street. Mrs Landemare, who had been married to a French chef, became legendary for what she could do with basic wartime provisions.

Clementine's presence at dinner enabled her on occasions to contradict her husband in the national interest. A tense meeting at Downing Street in mid-summer 1940 with the Free French leader General Charles de Gaulle took place in the small white dining room at Downing Street – much admired on his visit by Cecil Beaton – shortly after Winston had ordered the Royal Navy to open fire on the French fleet anchored at Oran in North Africa to prevent it from falling into enemy hands. When the conversation over lunch turned to the future of the remaining French fleet, Clementine said she hoped it would support the British effort to defeat the Nazis. De Gaulle

Clementine at Winston's side in 1940, shortly after he became Prime Minister. She was already noted for her style; soon the military top brass would come to understand her political significance as well.

One of several portraits by the society
photographer Sir Cecil Beaton taken
in Downing Street in 1940 to reflect
her growing popularity with the public.
Beaton described her as 'a bright, unspoilt
and girlish woman'.

caustically replied that it would give the French more satisfaction to turn
their guns on the British.

In stately French, Clementine upbraided him for uttering sentiments
ill-suited to an ally, let alone a guest. Noticing the sudden tension, Winston
attempted to placate the General: 'You must forgive my wife. *Elle parle trop
bien le français.*' Glaring at her husband, Clementine retorted, again in
French: 'Winston, it's not that at all. There are certain things that a woman
can say to a man which a man cannot say, and I am saying them to you,
General de Gaulle!' The Frenchman apologised repeatedly to his hostess
and the following day he sent her a huge bouquet of flowers.

Pamela, who witnessed the encounter, regarded Clementine as the only
person who could say 'No' to Winston 'and she did that often, often, often,
often … She was hard on herself but was also hard on him.'[14] In one sitting,
Clementine had faced down not only her husband, but another of the most
powerful men in the fragile alliance against Germany. She earned in the
process the undying respect of both.

•

The winter of 1940–41 appeared to be, in Winston's own phrase, the 'hour
of doom'.[15] France, Poland, Denmark, Norway, Belgium and Holland had
all fallen. Hitler's Luftwaffe bombers were flattening swathes of British
cities, his U-boats were sinking vital supply ships in the North Atlantic,
and all the while Japan was 'glowering on the other side of the globe'.[16]
American support was critical if Britain were to survive. But US public
opinion remained largely isolationist; by this stage, America's material
contribution amounted to little more than some semi-obsolete destroyers.
It was at this bleak point in history that President Roosevelt decided to send
to London a personal emissary – an ailing, gambling, wisecracking welfare
administrator of humble origins and virulent Anglo-sceptic views. He was
the first of a series of Americans to whom Clementine's ministrations would
be a significant means of promoting US involvement in the war.

Seduction USA

1941–42

Instinctively an isolationist, the sallow-faced and ailing Harry Hopkins seriously doubted whether Britain was even worth saving. Divorced from his first wife, bereft by the death of his second and having arrived in Britain during the damp chill of an English winter, he was in evident need of mothering. The decidedly un-maternal Clementine instantly took him under her wing.

Winston and Clementine, in her usual turban, on London's Horse Guards Parade after inspecting the American Mechanised Squadron on 9 January 1941.

Clementine took on many duties previously considered the preserve of men.
Here she is inspecting the Home Guard and awarding certificates for gallantry in July 1941.

A private lunch with Winston had been arranged for Hopkins, and in Downing Street Clementine was hard at work. She ensured that the wartime dining room in the basement looked as appealing as possible, despite the presence of steel shutters at the windows and metal pit props to strengthen the ceiling. The overall effect, enhanced by flowers and a prominently placed photograph of the alluring Pamela Churchill, as well as paintings by the French masters Ingres and David, was of a ship's wardroom. It was all part of the Churchills' joint campaign to win over Hopkins and his president to the cause through their own brand of persuasive charm. He was bowled over by Mrs Landemare's cooking as well as Clementine's personal attention – she even put a hot-water bottle in his bed at night after noticing how he was feeling the cold. Winston, of course, added his own force of personality to the potent mix.

Clementine planned virtually every moment of Hopkins' day with the aim of projecting the British and their hopes for victory in their best light. She made a 'great fuss' if the staff allowed him to stray from her carefully chosen itinerary for a moment. And as she had hoped, he was astonished by the good-humoured determination of a people he met on visits to bombsites, who lived with the constant reality of death and destruction. He was also moved by the enthusiastic welcome he received as the representative of a nation that had been miserly in its support for the last democracy in Europe to hold out against fascism. But for all this, Hopkins had no doubt that 'the most charming and entertaining of all the people that he met' on his entire six-week trip 'was Mrs Churchill'.[1]

Hopkins arrived back in the US 'more of a partisan than perhaps might have been expected by anyone who had not been exposed to the Churchillian force'.[2] He told Roosevelt that America must do all it could to help Britain with guns, ships and planes, as well as providing financial aid. Neither did he forget his hostess. He sent Clementine parcels of cheese, lipstick, ham, chocolate, bacon, a satin nightdress and nail polish.

Hopkins was not the only influential American to be won over by the Churchills' joint efforts. On his first night in London, he had dined with Ed Murrow, the resident CBS correspondent, who was then beaming the horror of the Blitz directly into American homes every night. Winston had long since identified Murrow as the conduit to the hearts and minds of US popular opinion; it was through Clementine's initiative, having spotted in Murrow's

•

Clementine planned virtually every moment of Hopkins' day with the aim of projecting the British and their hopes for victory in their best light.

•

Opposite: Clementine spent a great deal of time supporting voluntary schemes to help the home front. In July 1941, she visited a communal services kitchen in Fulham Road, London, with the mayor of Kensington.

wife the opportunity to cultivate the journalist, that the American was drawn into the Churchill fold.

A quiet Connecticut Yankee with a dislike of the English class system, Janet Murrow was a great influence on her husband, but was largely ignored by the men who dominated the powerful circles in which he moved. She was known to feel lonely in London, and Clementine had gone to work alongside her distributing American 'Bundles for Britain' aid parcels, during which time she had openly sympathised with many of Janet's radical views. Mrs Murrow in turn had been surprised and flattered by the attention.

Clementine rarely issued invitations to Downing Street on her own account, but she made an exception for Janet. And when Murrow arrived to collect his wife following one of her lunches with Clementine, Winston was presented with the perfect opportunity. Scuttling out from his study right on cue, he waved the American inside with the words, 'Good to see you. Have you time for several whiskies?'[3] It was an offer from the British Prime Minister that could scarcely be refused.

Murrow, moreover, was close friends with the new American ambassador. Gil Winant arrived at Bristol in March 1941 to discover a Britain enduring massive casualties from relentless air raids, devastating losses in the fighting overseas and the imminent threat of starvation as Germany's U-boats strangled the naval supply lines. As they had for Hopkins, the Churchills ensured that Winant's welcome was spectacular. He, too, was treated to an intimate dinner and thus was made another recruit to the greater Churchill 'family'. Winant became a familiar and reassuring figure on the Churchills' visits to bomb-damaged cities, where he was struck not only by the people's courage but by Clementine's unsung contribution. He noted to Roosevelt that women in particular showed 'great appreciation of Mrs Churchill's coming'.[4]

Clementine especially loved it when Winant came to visit. They were kindred spirits: both shy and reserved, each quietly radical, believing in a duty to help the less fortunate. Winant held Clementine's courage, resourcefulness, determination and devotion to the British people in the highest regard. Writing on one occasion to ask her to congratulate Winston on one of his speeches, 'the greatest of its kind ever made', he acknowledged her part in its success: 'I especially liked the references to de Gaulle and France and felt that, perhaps, you had had something to do with it.'[5] But it was another Churchill who was to capture his heart.

Winant noted to Roosevelt that women in particular
showed 'great appreciation of Mrs Churchill's coming'.

Glamorous, entertaining and alluring in her WAAF uniform, Sarah was enjoying her contribution to the war effort. Some elusive quality about her mesmerised Winant, who was frequently thrown into her company, and the pair, although both married, began an affair. Sarah's coy reference, years later, to a 'love affair which my father suspected but about which we did not speak'[6] belies her parents' acquiescence: the fraught situation of 1941 meant that almost any consolidation of Britain's 'special relationship' with America could be considered an act of patriotism. Though the Churchills may not have talked about it openly, they not only tolerated the affair but gave it plenty of opportunities to flourish.

At around the same time as Winant, Averell Harriman, a rich American Lothario with film-star looks, arrived in London to set up Roosevelt's new Lend-Lease military aid programme. Within days, Harriman was ostentatiously flattered by being given an office at the Admiralty, access to secret cables and invitations to high-level meetings. His wealth, looks and, most of all, power made him London's latest social catch; he was showered with invitations. One he was advised not to miss was a glamorous dinner at the Dorchester in April; there, seated next to him in a shoulderless gold dress, he was to find twenty-one-year-old Pamela Churchill.

For Pamela, Harriman was the most beautiful man she had ever seen. She had moreover been briefed that, as Roosevelt's special emissary, Harriman would be instrumental in deciding whether Britain won the war. So, over dinner, she launched into what friends came to call her 'mating dance'. She asked him questions, listened raptly to his answers, stroked his arm with her fingertips and laughed when he attempted a joke. After dinner, Harriman invited Pamela back to his palatial suite, where she helped him peel off her dress and where they lingered under the sheets throughout the night's heavy bombing. The building shook and the guns roared, but Pamela was ensconced in bed with the man who might just be able to help bring it all to an end. It was the first act of her career as the twentieth century's most influential courtesan.

Far from trying to stop the affair, it appears that Clementine ensured that Pamela and Harriman were thrust together as often as possible. Indeed, intimates of the Churchills such as the Duff Coopers thought that Winston and Clementine themselves were behind Pamela's subsequent activities. 'They set Pam up in a very luxurious flat … where her job was to give dinner parties to the top American brass and if necessary go to bed with them

Clementine especially loved it when Winant came to visit.
They were kindred spirits: both shy and reserved, each quietly
radical, believing in a duty to help the less fortunate.

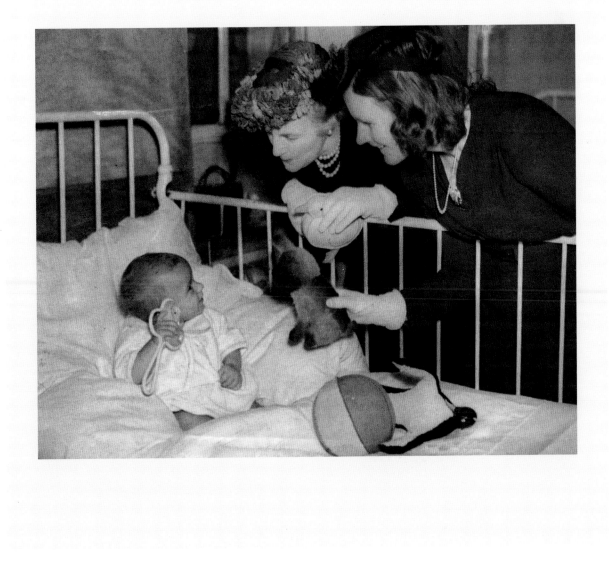

Clementine was widely praised for her practical and moral support for a number of wartime hospitals, including, but by no means only, the new Churchill Hospital at Oxford.

afterwards,' said John Julius Norwich, who remembered his parents discussing the matter.[7] Harriman and Winant were among many involved in love affairs with Churchills. And there can be little doubt that Winston and Clementine knew about these relationships, and good reason to believe that, for reasons of strategic necessity, they condoned them.

When Randolph came home on leave and discovered his wife's affair with Harriman, he exploded with rage. His anger stemmed not from sexual jealousy of Pamela, friends said, but more a sense of betrayal. He accused his parents of condoning adultery 'beneath their own roof' and sacrificing his marriage and happiness in order to woo the Americans. Their acceptance was not due to a moral permissiveness, however, but rather strategic necessity. For the sake of her country, Clementine would go to almost any lengths.

Clementine was now expert at preparing official receptions with military precision. A typical weekend at Chequers, for instance, would be arranged on a grid system and could easily involve twenty constantly changing guests coming and going, staying variously for lunch, dinner, overnight – or all three. Considering the circumstances, her hospitality was legendary. Clementine was not only intent on keeping Winston happily fed. She also studied their countless visitors' backgrounds, families, interests and tastes in food – having discovered Eisenhower's love of stew, Clementine ensured he was served the finest (with plenty of onions!) – and took great care over her seating plans to ensure everyone's compatibility and comfort. Meals at Downing Street, Chequers or Ditchley were a much-needed, spirit-lifting spectacle, as well as a stage on which Winston could work his magic on his carefully selected guests.

The Churchills also made an impression through their eccentric attire. Winston liked to wear a siren suit at dinner – a bizarre onesie-style garment that Clementine had made up for him in a variety of colours and fabrics, including velvet. She, by contrast, presided over more intimate dinners in beautiful flowery silk housecoats with her nightdress underneath. As Gil Winant observed, their world even in war was never dull or drab, but forever 'shot through with colour'.

Yet despite her hard work few visitors paused to register, let alone admire, Clementine's efforts. One rare exception was the Canadian Prime Minister Mackenzie King, who told her that he 'marvelled' at how 'you are able to *think* of the many things you do, to say nothing of how you manage to perform them'.[8] The Churchills' outward charm and energy belied, of course,

> Clementine was now expert at preparing official receptions with military precision. A typical weekend at Chequers, for instance, would be arranged on a grid system and could easily involve twenty constantly changing guests coming and going.

the strain two long years of war had taken on them. Moreover, their frantic dinner-table diplomacy had yet to yield the ultimate prize. What would it take, Winston and Clementine wondered, to propel Roosevelt to lead his country into battle at their side?

•

> Exhausted by her relentless workload and family worries, and plagued by bouts of bronchitis, Clementine had not taken a significant break since the summer of 1939.

Exhausted by her relentless workload and family worries, and plagued by bouts of bronchitis, Clementine had not taken a significant break since the summer of 1939. So when Winston finally received an invitation from Roosevelt to discuss the war at a summit in Placentia Bay, Newfoundland, in August 1941, she seized her chance for a respite and checked herself into a 'Nature Cure' clinic. Today, Champneys in Hertfordshire is a beauty clinic and spa offering conventional medical services, but in the 1940s, Dr Lief's establishment had a reputation for strange 'electrical' appliances and putting its patients into padded cells where they were 'starved and hosed and worse'.[9]

Dr Lief was undoubtedly concerned about his VIP patient. Upon her return home, he advised her to take a day off from her duties every week, but though 'rest days' were duly marked in her diary for the next couple of months the idea was unsustainable. Even so, when she went to greet Winston at London's King's Cross station on 19 August, she felt much revived, and the news from his summit gave her cause for optimism. Along with Roosevelt, he had signed the Atlantic Charter, outlining their joint hopes for the post-war world. The President had resisted committing to the US entering the war, but surely that could not now be long?

Four months later, on the night of Sunday 7 December, the closest of the Churchills' circle gathered for dinner at Chequers. The mood was glum: news from the front was relentlessly bad and yet America was still stalling. Around nine, Winston's butler, Sawyers, carried in a little radio and switched it on for the BBC news, just in time to catch a momentous announcement: 'Japanese aircraft have raided Pearl Harbor, the American naval base in Hawaii.'[10] The very next day, Winston started to make plans to visit Roosevelt in Washington DC. After crossing the Atlantic through a series of terrific gales, Winston stayed at the White House over Christmas, where he and the President often talked long into the night.

The Churchills are visiting an anti-aircraft battery, where women served alongside men as predictors and range-fighters. Clementine is wearing her trademark turban.

Two First Ladies of war: Eleanor Roosevelt was keen to drag Clementine into the limelight with
her and here they are broadcasting together in Quebec in September 1944. Clementine admired
Eleanor's easy, chatty style and public works but Winston was not such a fan.

Unlike Winston, Roosevelt was not a one-woman man. He chose to surround himself with adoring and undemanding admirers, referred to by his wife, Eleanor, as his 'handmaidens'. Her discovery, in 1918, of his affair with her beautiful social secretary, Lucy Mercer, had made Eleanor fiercely independent, and their subsequent partnership was professional rather than intimate. When Franklin could not attend speeches or rallies in the 1920s because of his ill health, Eleanor stood in for him; she became one of the first great female voices of the Democratic party. She had also acted as the President's eyes and ears during his administration's battle to implement the New Deal welfare plan in response to the 1930s' American Depression.

By the time the US entered the war, Eleanor was fifty-seven and age had not been kind to her. Her wavy brown hair was flecked with grey; her buck teeth and receding chin detracted from her dazzling blue eyes. Nearly six foot tall, she dominated a room but did not conform to Winston's ideas of 'attractive', while she was uninterested in fripperies such as good food, décor or even her own dress. Yet for her devotion to the American people, the energy she expended on their behalf and her unfailingly sharp-minded and wholesome public image, she often enjoyed higher approval ratings than her husband.

America's entry into the war in December 1941 – however heartening – did nothing immediately to stem discontent at home in Britain. In January 1942, criticism of the government's prosecution of the war led to a vote of confidence in the Commons. Winston won by 464 to 1, but that success still failed to silence the critics. And worse was yet to come. On 15 February 1942, the Japanese took Singapore after the surrender of 60,000 British troops – a defeat Winston himself described as the worst disaster and largest capitulation in British history. Clementine fretted about the effect this latest ignominy would have on his already battered morale.

Winston defiantly won another confidence vote in July 1942, but his speech to the House offered a rare glimpse of his own suffering – an admission that bore all the signs of Clementine's gift for reading the public mood: 'Some people assume too readily that, because a Government keeps cool and has steady nerves under reverses, its members do not feel the public misfortunes as keenly as its independent critics,' he said. 'On the contrary, I doubt whether anyone feels greater sorrow or pain than those who are responsible for the general conduct of our affairs.'

Family grievances also weighed heavily on the Churchills at this time – not least Randolph's bitterness towards them. One night in spring 1942, father

•

Clementine took particular pains to ensure Winston was on his best behaviour when they welcomed Eleanor Roosevelt to Britain at the end of October.

•

and son rowed so violently about Pamela's affair with Harriman that Clementine feared Winston might have a seizure; she banned Randolph from Downing Street for the rest of the war.

•

Clementine took particular pains to ensure Winston was on his best behaviour when they welcomed Eleanor Roosevelt to Britain at the end of October. Once again, they pulled out all the stops: after spending her first few days with the King and Queen, Eleanor was to join Winston and Clementine for a weekend at Chequers. It was the first time these redoubtable women had met and both were curious about the other. They certainly looked different: Clementine beautiful and immaculate; Eleanor plain and slightly windswept. More significantly, their public personas stood in marked contrast: Clementine avoided voicing her views publicly and remained at her husband's side almost throughout the war, whereas Eleanor maximised her own status, travelled widely without the President and confidently aired her own opinions in newspaper columns. She was frequently credited with having become the 'most influential woman of her age'.[11]

These apparent differences masked numerous parallels in their lives. They were of a similar age and upper-class background; they shared a concern for the poor and a dislike of gambling and extravagance that led some to consider them 'crashing bores'. They had endured difficult and fearful childhoods and as girls had been considered plain. Their lives had been touched by family tragedy and left them plagued by self-doubt, sometimes even depression. Like Clementine, Eleanor thought herself an inadequate mother and she had lost a child in infancy.

They also shared the chronic loneliness and isolation that often afflicts the wives of ambitious men. Winston and Franklin were implacable optimists who, in some ways, had never entirely grown up. Now Fate had chosen them to carry the immense burden of saving the world and neither man's spouse found her supporting role easy.

Eleanor had never wanted to be First Lady and yet there was much in Clementine that *did* want to be married to the Prime Minister, although it was tempered by her insecurity. The two women were keepers of their

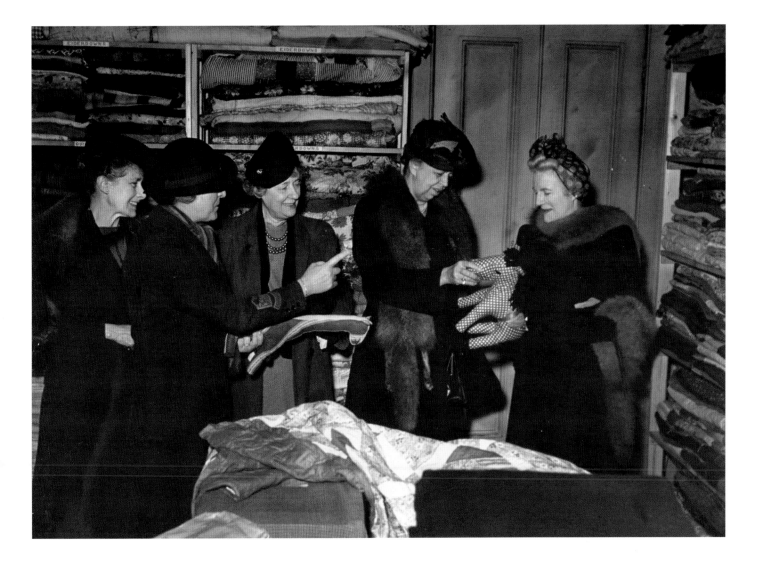

Eleanor Roosevelt came to Britain on an official visit in 1942. She and Clementine, pictured with her here, were to become friends and often stepped in when necessary to patch up the vital wartime Anglo-American alliance.

Clementine avoided voicing
her views publicly and remained
at her husband's side almost
throughout the war

Although naturally shy, Clementine forced
herself to take a prominent role and recruited
many from all walks of life to help the war effort
through her charm and perseverance. Here she
is visiting the Bedfordshire home of Lord and
Lady Milchett, which had been turned into a rest
centre for nurses from bombed-out areas.

Clementine thought it important to look glamorous and cheerful on her public visits (however she was feeling inside) to denote optimism and confidence in victory. Here she is chatting with Aid to Russia Fund volunteers based at Derry & Toms department store in Kensington. 16 December 1941.

husbands' consciences, safeguarding the 'ordinary' citizen's interests. Ultimately, however, one was to prove considerably more influential during the war than the other.

On 23 October 1942, Eleanor arrived at Paddington station in west London, where a large crowd had gathered to greet her. At Buckingham Palace, she was put in an enormous suite, specially restored after a bombing raid. She was also given her own ration card and assigned a bed in the converted cellar that served as a royal air-raid shelter. British women struggling with severe clothing rations warmed to Eleanor's lack of ostentatious chic. She came over as more homely than Clementine – more believably of the people – and she was refreshingly informal. She instantly called Clementine's secretary, Grace Hamblin, by her first name – an unimaginable familiarity in the Churchill household until that point – and thereafter Clementine (but not Winston) followed suit.

As ever, Eleanor drowned her insecurities in a punishing work schedule. Clementine observed how the American First Lady was a celebrity in her own right, prompting spontaneous outbursts of cheering wherever she went. In Oxford, Cambridge, Bristol, Birmingham, Manchester, Liverpool, Glasgow, Belfast and Edinburgh, she received standing ovations. In London, people loitered around the American Embassy just to get a glimpse of her. Her enthusiasm never seemed to flag, and she soon outpaced not only the posse of 'saggy-kneed' reporters who trailed her every move, but also Clementine herself. On one visit, Mrs Churchill was left to sit and rest on a marble staircase while Mrs Roosevelt ran up four flights to chat to more workers. She went out of her way, through mud and rain, to meet the former hairdressers, typists and housewives who were now digging ditches, servicing planes and driving tractors.

Eleanor was also impressed by the legions of female volunteers who had stepped up to staff hostels, mobile libraries and canteens or to spruce up shelters and distribute the thousands of tonnes of clothing and other supplies collected from America and the Commonwealth. The huge and unconventional role of British women in wartime had become the norm through necessity, but Eleanor's praise lent it dignity, glamour even. It was all enormously gratifying for her British counterpart, who had done so much to bring women into the war. Their contribution, in a country whose attitudes had previously seemed so conservative, appears to have struck many Americans – and helped to convince them that Britain really might prevail.

•

The huge and unconventional role of British women in wartime had become the norm through necessity.

•

Clementine's mailbag was huge. Thousands of letters poured in every week from people offering help for her Aid to Russia fund. Some sent cash, others knitted gloves or jumpers for those on the front line. In all, she raised the equivalent of £350 million today from a country suffering its own dire shortages.

•

For the rest of the war, she was to push herself
forward in a way that would have been
unthinkable before.

•

Eleanor, meanwhile, found Clementine attractive, youthful and charming
but constrained by her husband's notion that women should stay in the
background. She saw that Clementine worked diligently to support relief
efforts for Russia and China, but also observed that she was 'very careful
not to voice any opinions publicly or to associate with any political
organisations'.[12] There were occasional flashes of tension between Winston
and Clementine, however, that might suggest she welcomed Eleanor's
willingness to challenge him. At a small dinner party held in Mrs Roosevelt's
honour, the Prime Minister brought up the subject of Spain. Eleanor asked
why it had not been possible to help the anti-fascists. Winston replied that
they would have been the first to lose their heads if the Spanish republicans
had won; Eleanor countered that she did not care if she lost her head.
Incensed by a woman confronting him in public, Winston fired back: 'I don't
want you to lose your head and neither do I want to lose mine!' At this point,
Clementine leaned across the table and said pointedly, 'I think perhaps Mrs
Roosevelt is right.' An astonished Winston rose abruptly from the table,
signalling that dinner was over.

Clementine may well have intervened for strategic reasons – ensuring that
their important visitor was not offended and understanding that the trans-
Atlantic alliance was of paramount importance. Yet there is no doubt that a
bond formed between the two women. Neither was the influence entirely
one-sided: when Eleanor got home, she took an hour and a half out of her
frenetic work schedule to have her hair and nails done. Clementine herself,
moreover, had watched and learned. For the rest of the war, she was to push
herself forward in a way that would have been unthinkable before.

From FDR to Stalin

1943–45

It was an almost intolerable burden to bear alone. Winston had already suffered a minor heart attack during his stay with Roosevelt – one which his doctor, Lord Moran, desperate not to jeopardise the success of the summit, kept even from Winston himself. Now, what Moran had to tell Clementine in January 1943 was devastating. Winston's worsening heart condition meant he might suffer a critical coronary thrombosis at any moment. Knowing what this might mean for Winston's ability to continue conducting the war, Moran had decided he must seek instruction from Clementine: should the Prime Minister be informed of the seriousness of his condition, or should he deliberately be kept in the dark?

Clementine believed strongly that women playing a variety of roles were key to winning the war and was instrumental in breaking down barriers for them.

Clementine took the decision: Winston must be allowed to carry on unencumbered by fears for his own life, in particular the many risky plane journeys entailed in his frantic round of wartime diplomacy. He had begun in 1943 by flying 1,300 miles, for instance, in an unheated bomber to meet Roosevelt in Casablanca. She would make no attempt to dissuade her husband from his travels; often (provided Moran accompanied him) she would applaud them. In this she thought, first and foremost, of what was best for her country; she redoubled her efforts to care for Winston, but kept the awful truth of his condition to herself. It was arguably her most decisive – and courageous – act of the war.

Clementine made a point of waiting, beautifully dressed and smiling, to welcome Winston whenever he arrived home from his travels, and his return from North Africa on 7 February 1943 was no exception. On this occasion, their reunion did little to quell her unease. Winston returned unwell – with a nagging cold and a look of utter weariness – and less than a fortnight later, during one of the rare occasions when they were dining alone together during the war, he became seriously ill. He was diagnosed with pneumonia. Despite her worry, Clementine continued to keep a brave face.

In between, Clementine rushed off to fulfil her own official duties. Two years earlier, she had become president of the Young Women's Christian Association's Wartime Appeal. The YWCA provided hostels, clubs and canteens for women war workers and the rising numbers of servicewomen. Clementine had started making broadcast appeals for donations on the BBC, at first sticking rigidly to someone else's script, but over time gaining in confidence and putting more of herself into the messages.

It was her appeal for the Red Cross Aid to Russia Fund, however – originally launched back in October 1941 – that was to become perhaps her greatest work. It not only helped to cement the uneasy alliance between Britain and Soviet Russia, but also quelled anger at home that the government was not doing more to help a people being butchered by their Nazi invaders. By Christmas that year, she had already raised £1 million, and buoyed by this success, she increasingly pushed herself forward to maintain the momentum. She recruited factory workers, millionaires and widows; she organised auctions, flag days and galas, and persuaded celebrity musicians to give concerts. She also presided over home nations football matches in aid of her fund. In February 1943, England's 5–3 triumph over Wales raised the bar

OF THE NATIONAL COUNCIL OF WOMEN

for charity fundraising events to a new height, bringing in £12,500 in a single day. In all, the donations eventually totalled £8 million (some £300 million in today's money).

It was an extraordinary achievement on a global scale. Soon hundreds of thousands of tonnes of medical supplies were on their way to Russia from a country itself struggling desperately with shortages. Meanwhile, Clementine worked closely with Agnes Maisky, the imperious wife of the Soviet ambassador. It was a meeting of two volatile and patriotic women and produced plenty of fireworks, but thanks to Clementine's diplomatic charm and efficiency, ultimately a useful strategic friendship was forged.

Clementine, in trademark turban and coat, worked closely with the Young Women's Christian Association during the war to ensure that young, single female workers were well looked after. Here she is the first customer of the mobile club vans she presented to the YWCA.

Clementine consults a chart of the contributions to her spectacularly successful appeal for the Red Cross Aid to Russia Fund. 23 May 1944.

Meanwhile, Winston had come away from his latest visit to Washington a reduced figure in Roosevelt's eyes. Now that American money, forces and firepower were flooding into the war, the President saw himself as the senior partner in the alliance and expected to have his way. Nonetheless, after a month in the US Winston arrived back in London on 5 June feeling revitalised. Overall, the war was moving in Britain's favour. The consequent lifting of the strain permitted the Churchills a little time for entertainment. They played bezique, at which the strategically minded Clementine roundly beat him, and they went to the theatre, taking in two new plays by Noël Coward: *This Happy Breed* and *Present Laughter*.

In August 1943, Clementine broke with tradition by accompanying her husband when he set off to Quebec for yet another conference with Roosevelt. Sensing his own influence over Roosevelt was waning, Winston hoped that Clementine would be able to use her powers to good use with the President. Upon receiving word from Winston that Clementine and her daughter would be attending, the President cabled back, 'I am perfectly delighted.'[1]

On 10 August, the Churchills arrived in Canada on board the *Queen Mary* and were taken to the Citadel, the fortified royal residence on the cliffs above the Saint Lawrence river. That evening Clementine gazed out across Quebec and, after four years of blackout, marvelled at the sight of twinkling lights. But she felt too dog-tired to enjoy it for long; physically and mentally drained, she feared she would let Winston down at the conference. As a result, she turned down Roosevelt's invitation to spend a few days at Hyde Park, New York, his country estate over the border, instead staying behind at the Citadel. Mercifully, by the time he and Mary returned to Quebec, she appeared to be back on form.

Roosevelt is unlikely to have noticed anything remiss when he finally met her on 17 August 1943, although for her part Clementine was disappointed by the man whom her husband so adored. His easy charm usually won over detractors but had the opposite effect on her. His greatest crime appears to have been that he took the 'liberty' of addressing her as 'Clemmie', a privilege

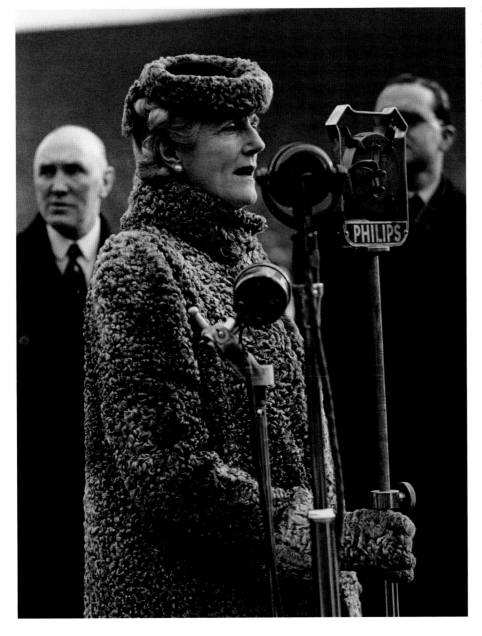

Clementine wearing her trademark coat when addressing an England v Scotland football match at Wembley in 1942. The event raised thousands for her Aid to Russia Fund.

normally reserved for only the most deserving and long-serving friends. Over dinner one night Roosevelt was to transgress again when the names of Sarah Churchill and the President's son, Elliott, cropped up in conversation. He leant over to Clementine and whispered conspiratorially: 'Wouldn't it be wonderful if something happened between those two?' Bristling with rage, she drew herself up and retorted: 'Mr President, I have to point out to you that they are both married to other people!'[2] This moralistic 'Clemmie' was never likely to appeal to Roosevelt.

Fortunately, she was more successful in winning over the American people. On 2 September, she attracted generous notices for her first ever press conference, which she held by herself to great acclaim. The *Washington Times Herald* hailed her as 'Winston's greatest asset'; she was described as 'witty, daring and direct' and a 'brilliant platform speaker'. Was England becoming dowdy in the war?, she was asked. She had not thought so, she replied – dressed in shimmering black silk – 'until I came to America!' Clementine was proving herself a public triumph in Washington at a time when – apart from Eleanor Roosevelt – most leaders' wives were barely seen, let alone heard. She had always been accident-prone when stretched, however, and this visit was no exception. On her last day in town, she fell down some steps in a bookshop and cracked her elbow. She left the capital with her arm in a sling and in considerable pain.

Clementine seems to have had regrets about missing the first of the so-called 'Big Three' gatherings with Stalin, held in November 1943 at the Soviet legation in Tehran. But it was perhaps fortunate she stayed behind as she kept a steady hand on the rudder at home. She reviewed reports on parliamentary debates, read the most secret telegrams, kept Winston's deputy, Clement Attlee, informed of the Prime Minister's progress, dealt with constituency matters and sent Winston digests of public reaction to the war. And, from afar, she exerted an influence at the conference, too. No less distrustful of Roosevelt than before, she counselled her husband to be wary in how he handled the President. She understood the strategic imperative of befriending Roosevelt, but she also thought Winston sentimental and emotionally transparent. She warned him to be more guarded. Now he was to discover the real nature of his 'friendship' with the President. Tehran was the moment Roosevelt clearly chose Stalin over Winston.

After six weeks with a heavy cold, in Tehran Winston asked his doctor: 'Do you think my strength will last out the war? I fancy sometimes that I am

nearly spent.'³ Yet despite the ordeal of the conference, Moran failed to persuade him to abandon a flight to Tunis to see the American commander, General Eisenhower. By the time Winston reached Eisenhower's white, cube-shaped villa near ancient Carthage, the Prime Minister was feeling so ill he went straight to bed. The next morning, he was diagnosed with pneumonia again and a seriously fibrillating heart.

Alarmed that Winston might die at any moment, the Cabinet secretly requested Clementine to fly out to be by his side. She packed to leave at once, knowing full well that the crisis she had so feared since January was finally upon them. The only available plane was an unheated Liberator bomber, but with the news from Carthage still worsening Clementine could not afford to wait. Fortunately the bomb-racks had already been removed, so a few RAF rugs were hastily spread on the floor while Clementine was zipped into a flight suit ready for take-off. Colville remembered her seeming 'gay and

Winston gives the 'V' sign to cheering troops in September 1943 while Clementine beams.

•

Alarmed that Winston might die at any moment, the Cabinet secretly requested Clementine to fly out to be by his side. She packed to leave at once.

•

apparently unconcerned'; she later admitted to Mary, however, that she had been so frightened her knees had been knocking together.

Though Clementine was exhausted once they were in the air, the fears inside her head made sleep impossible; no doubt she revisited many times her decision not to tell Winston about his heart condition. But her only option was courage: she dug into her luggage and produced a backgammon board. Draped in blankets to keep out the perishing cold and sustained by black coffee, Clementine and Colville played at least thirty games during that long, slow flight.

Winston's condition meanwhile was still deteriorating and privately his doctors wondered whether his wife would arrive in time. When she finally reached Carthage on 17 December, however, her presence had an extraordinary effect. Winston was soon able to send Mary a soothing message: 'Your Mother is here. All is joyful. No need to worry.'[4]

With Clementine on hand, Winston was soon able to work in bed, summoning assistants and giving orders almost as normal. John Martin, one of his private secretaries, observed just how important she was to his ability to go on. 'Above all, Churchill was sustained in storm and stress,' he judged, 'because his life was rooted in such a happy marriage.'[5]

When Winston finally appeared to be out of danger, the couple left for a period of convalescence at Villa Taylor, near the Mamounia Hotel in Marrakech. Meanwhile, Clementine resorted to every conceivable ploy to boost Winston's strength. They went on picnics in the Atlas foothills, and at last Winston felt sufficiently strong to climb up a large boulder. Diana Cooper observed that Clementine said nothing, 'but watched him with me like a lenient mother who does not wish to spoil her child's fun nor yet his daring'.

•

While Winston had lain gravely ill in Morocco, a crisis had been brewing among his allies. France for both Winston and Clementine was of special emotional significance; their shared love of l'Hexagone had helped to bring them together. But the prickly General de Gaulle had caused Winston apoplexy with a 'boorish' and clearly unappreciative message and now the

Frenchman announced he was on his way for what threatened to be a stormy encounter. 'I am trying to smooth Papa down,' Clementine anxiously reported to the family, although she was also lecturing him to avoid antagonising de Gaulle unnecessarily. 'I hope there will be no explosions!'[6]

When the French leader arrived, she quickly diverted him away from his aides and into the garden, where she could speak frankly. Sarah overheard part of the conversation, during which Clementine remarked pointedly: 'Mon Général, you must take care not to hate your allies more than your enemies.'[7] The subsequent lunch and discussions played out more amicably than expected, with de Gaulle most unusually insistent on speaking English. There can have been few – if any – other figures with such powerful sway over a notoriously truculent leader.

On 18 January 1944, Clementine made her next appearance in the House of Commons' gallery. Although Winston was now fit enough to resume his

Churchill liked to travel in comfort and arrive in luxury. Here he is travelling in the train lent to him in the 1940s for his journeys across the US and Canada. The specially-appointed carriages allowed the Churchills to keep working along with their secretaries.

prime ministerial duties, Clementine's presence reflected her concern – based on her ever-accurate political antennae – about the reception he might receive. And her fears were justified. Smiling down at him as he entered the chamber, she saw the House rise to cheer him. But, as the MP Henry 'Chips' Channon reported, the welcome, for a man who had cheated death, was merely 'courteous', even 'curiously cold'.

•

By the spring of 1944, Britain was in a state of alert for the planned D-Day landings. Despite Winston's misgivings, it was clear that Operation Overlord – as the invasion of northern France was codenamed – was the inescapable next move in the conflict. And whereas Roosevelt waited until the evening before the invasion to brief Eleanor on the plan, he had shared the details – and the dangers – of Operation Overlord with Clementine from the beginning. Fortunately, the King had joined her in opposing Winston's plan to watch the battle unfold from the bridge of the cruiser HMS *Belfast*, and the Prime Minister was forced to count down the final hours back in London.

On the day itself, Winston lunched with His Majesty; Clementine meanwhile ate with the head of the Army, Alan Brooke. The tension in the ensuing hours and days was unprecedented and she witnessed its emotional and physical toll not only on Winston but also on General Eisenhower, now supreme commander, who was smoking and drinking too much and suffering from headaches, recurring throat infections, sky-rocketing blood pressure and low spirits. She tried to help both in any way she could. By the time Winston finally reached the beachhead of liberated France on 12 June, however, it was becoming clear that the operation – although not yet complete – had been a success.

From the fall of France, in June 1940, until December 1941, when America entered the war, Clementine had always been there to chivvy Winston along, even at his lowest points, as he carried the fate of Europe and the British Empire on his shoulders. Now, one evening at Chequers in June 1944, just after the successful landings in Normandy, when Winston announced despondently that he was 'an old and weary man', she responded brightly: 'But think what Hitler and Mussolini feel like!'[8] By that summer, though, with

Britain's survival no longer in doubt, 'it was plain that he was nearly burnt out'.[9]

With the liberation of Europe, moreover, came increasing discontent on the Home Front. When, upon visiting Britain in August 1944, Roosevelt's Treasury Secretary Henry Morgenthau asked to take a tour of air-raid shelters, no one could think of a single senior government figure sufficiently popular to escort him without inciting protests. Eventually, Clementine emerged as the obvious and only choice.[10] Morgenthau watched her in action: smiling, listening, raising spirits and providing practical help. Her easy, personable, almost motherly style was now suddenly familiar. 'The dame is unbelievable … She is like Mrs Roosevelt!'[11]

August 1944 brought the liberation of Paris. With Winston away in Italy, Jock Colville accompanied Clementine on the 27th to a service at St Paul's Cathedral to give thanks. Feeling Winston's absence keenly, two days later she was at Northolt air base to greet him on his return, but when the plane landed a frantic Moran emerged, yelling that his patient had a raging temperature of 103° with a patch on his lung. Clementine was once again 'sick with fright'. In just six days, Winston was due to depart for the second Quebec conference with Roosevelt. Winston had already briefed Clementine on what he needed to achieve and made it clear that her presence would be a 'pleasure' but also a 'help' in achieving this goal.[12] Knowing the matter to be delicate, he had informed Roosevelt of her attendance in advance. The President had cabled back: 'Perfectly delighted … Eleanor will go with me.'

Determined to avoid the mistakes of the previous Quebec conference, Clementine stayed on her best behaviour, and made a strenuous effort to ensure that Winston was on his. There were new stresses at this summit caused by Roosevelt's fading health. His doctors were especially keen to deter him from taking part in late-night drinking sessions with Winston, and even the Americans realised the best way of achieving this was by enlisting Clementine's help. One evening, after the two parties watched a movie together, she duly took her husband firmly by the arm and steered him to bed.

On 17 September, the Churchills left to spend a few days at Hyde Park. Judging that Roosevelt's frailty meant his mind was no longer 'pinpointed' on the war for more than four hours a day, and hoping to reintroduce some sparkle to the Anglo-American relationship, Clementine made sure to spend as much time with his daughter, Anna, and Eleanor as possible. The women

•

Determined to avoid the mistakes of the previous Quebec conference, Clementine stayed on her best behaviour, and made a strenuous effort to ensure that Winston was on his.

•

179

Clementine (far left) introduced the idea of wives attending conferences of international leaders. Eleanor Roosevelt (second from right) was keen to follow suit and attended the second Quebec conference in 1944. President Roosevelt is third from left, with Churchill in the centre.

made brave attempts to paper over the cracks in the alliance between their two countries, to try to make up for the growing distance between Roosevelt and Winston. Yet for all the 'blaze of friendship' described by Winston, the second Quebec conference achieved little. On 20 September, their main strategic differences with the US still unaddressed, the Churchills boarded the *Queen Mary* for home.

Two days later, from on-board ship, a determined Clementine renewed her diplomatic overtures. She sent Eleanor a letter that was quite out of character in its gushing familiarity and one that demonstrated her diplomatic sensibilities. 'I shall always remember my delightful visit to Hyde Park,' she wrote, 'the picnics, sitting near the president, & my two long walks with you through your woods.' She closed by forecasting that in the forthcoming election, which she knew Roosevelt feared he was going to lose, 'your great country will honour itself by yet again returning its great leader'.[13] Now was not the time for any further cooling of relations. Clementine was well aware that Britain had become dependent on her former colony, not only to help bring the war to an end but to help her survive economically in the peace thereafter. She was now playing a deeply strategic role.

•

On 10 November, at the invitation of Charles de Gaulle, Winston and Clementine flew to Paris to celebrate the city's liberation. The scenes were unforgettable: crowds on pavements, balconies and rooftops cheered their heroes under a dazzling blue sky and a protective umbrella of Spitfires.

But the joy of Paris was not to last. In exercising greater powers than any other British leader of modern times, Winston had become accustomed to unquestioning obedience. In early 1944, he had even entertained the idea of becoming Foreign Secretary as well as Prime Minister and Minister of Defence – until it became clear that Clementine was implacably opposed to the idea. As the war entered its final months, patience was running out. On a snowy Saturday in January 1945, with Winston restricted to Downing Street by a heavy cold, Clement Attlee wrote to him protesting about the Prime Minister's 'lengthy disquisitions' in Cabinet on papers that he had not read and subjects that he had 'not taken the trouble to master'. He railed about Winston's 'undue attentiveness' to Bracken and Beaverbrook, whose views – 'often entirely ignorant' – were given more weight than the 'considered opinion' of Cabinet committees. Winston exploded with rage and drafted a viciously sarcastic reply in which Attlee's intervention was denounced as a 'socialist conspiracy'.[14]

In high dudgeon, Winston brought Attlee's letter to Clementine expecting her comforting support. He was greatly surprised to find that she took Attlee's side and thought the Deputy Prime Minister's missive 'true and wholesome'. The previous brutal response was duly discarded, and he sat down to write Attlee 'a short, polite acknowledgement'.[15] Her intervention had pre-empted what could have become a disastrous rift.

At the time of Attlee's protest, Winston was preparing for yet another conference of the Big Three. At Yalta, a few days later, he, Roosevelt and Stalin agreed a joint communiqué proclaiming the Allies' intention to strive for a peace in which 'all the men in all the lands may live out their lives in freedom from fear and want'. However, Winston knew that Stalin was acting out a lie; Clementine was his confidante as he wrote despondently, 'the misery of the whole world appalls me', and of his fears that 'new struggles may arise out of those we are successfully ending'.[16]

While Winston's star was falling at home and abroad, Clementine's was rising fast – and she was about to embark on her most independent and exciting venture yet. She was invited by the Soviet Red Cross to visit Russia in April to see the results of her fundraising – and it transpired that Stalin wanted to honour her by thanking her in person for her work. But with relations between Britain and the Soviet Union – over Poland in particular – becoming increasingly icy, Winston hesitated to let her go. Nor could she entirely conquer her anxiety about leaving him for so long. Before her departure she wrote to Mary: 'Darling supposing anything happened to me (e.g. air crash) Do you think you could be released from the ATS on Compassionate grounds to look after Papa?'[17]

Clementine's friendship with Clement Attlee survived his replacing Winston as Prime Minister in July 1945. Attlee went out of his way to be kind to her and she rated him as a shrewd deputy to her husband during the war.

Nevertheless, this was a singular and rare personal honour, and the trip might also reap diplomatic dividends. In any case she had already learned some Russian and had a Red Cross uniform altered so that it did not make her 'look like an elephant'. So she went; knowing she would be spending her sixtieth birthday away from him, Winston gave her a diamond-encrusted, heart-shaped brooch.

Having disembarked from her plane in Moscow pristine in her blue uniform, Clementine was presented with a large bouquet of roses by the reception party, which included Foreign Minister Molotov, as well as Ivan and Agnes Maisky and Averell Harriman. Touring hospitals from Leningrad to Stalingrad (all equipped courtesy of her Red Cross Fund) and receiving a Soviet Red Cross Distinguished Service Medal for her 'exceptional' contribution to the Russian war effort, Clementine delighted in being the centre of attention. Cheering crowds greeted her everywhere, dancers at the ballet applauded her, onlookers threw bunches of violets at her feet. She cuddled children, posed for photographs, and chatted in snippets of Russian with as many as she could. She even gave a press conference. Back home, reports of her astonishing popularity made Winston burst with pride. 'My darling one … Your personality reaches the gt masses & touches their heart.'[18] He told her she was the one and only 'bright-spot' in Anglo-Russian relations.

On 7 April, she received an invitation to meet Stalin himself at the Kremlin. Clementine, her Red Cross secretary, Mabel Johnson, and Grace Hamblin were led by their Red Army escort down 'long impressive corridors' until they came to a great double door. Once on the other side, Clementine and Johnson – Grace had not been permitted to enter – could see the stocky figure of Stalin, flanked by Molotov, behind a writing desk at the far end of a vast and imposing room. They walked to the desk where, speaking through an interpreter, Stalin thanked Clementine for the work done by her fund. She knew that Winston was hoping for a great deal from this meeting; having taken advice from the ambassador, she presented Stalin with a gold fountain pen, saying: 'My husband wishes me to express the hope that you will write him many friendly messages with it.' Stalin was not to be won so easily by a Churchill who had won the hearts of his own people. He put the pen to one side, muttering that he wrote only with a pencil.

Despite such indications of the souring of relations, Clementine continued to receive a rapturous welcome from Russians everywhere. In one military hospital equipped by her fund, she was 'visibly moved' when wounded men

●

She was invited by the Soviet Red Cross to visit Russia in April to see the results of her fundraising – and it transpired that Stalin wanted to honour her by thanking her in person for her work.

●

lined the stairways and corridors to bid her farewell. But for all her skilful charm, she was also determined to make further waves over the growing evidence of the Soviets' brutality and treachery, on one occasion giving Maisky one of her famous dressings down. Eleanor Rathbone, an Independent MP with a keen interest in Poland, had written to her in Moscow about the large number of Poles being deported to Soviet labour camps. Upon her return to London in May, she would write back to Rathbone, making plain her view that the West should 'break off Diplomatic relations' with Moscow if 'they do not mend their ways'. She added, in a handwritten annotation to this line, 'Winston would disapprove!'[19]

Nevertheless, away from the Kremlin, she particularly enjoyed the spontaneous post-dinner singing in Leningrad, during which her hosts were surprised to discover that she knew the 'Song of the Volga Boatmen'. It was here that she learned Stalin was to award her the prestigious Order of the Red Banner of Labour. But, when she returned to Moscow on her private train on 13 April, Molotov informed her of the shocking news that Roosevelt was dead. The cable she later sent to Eleanor (via the British ambassador in Washington) is surprisingly flat, as if in her shock she resorted to the safest option: 'I am deeply grieved and send my respectful sympathy and my thoughts. Clementine Churchill.' It was Winston who struck the right note: 'Accept my most profound sympathy in your grievous loss which is also the loss of the British Nation and of the cause of freedom in every land … I trust you may find consolation in the magnitude of his work and the glory of his name.'

Clementine's last few days in the Soviet Union were packed with more concerts, hospital tours and receptions in her honour, 'All my thoughts are with you on this supreme day my darling,' she cabled Winston on VE Day, 8 May 1945. 'It could not have happened without you.'[20] While Winston addressed the jubilant crowds from a balcony overlooking Whitehall, Clementine personally arranged a simultaneous party at the embassy in Moscow. She grabbed a glass of champagne and climbed onto a chair, declaring, 'We will drink to victory!'

Clementine's 'eyes open' tour had been, in personal terms, a triumph. After six weeks apart, Winston was there to greet her in person when she arrived at Northolt on 12 May. Clementine emerged, still wearing her Red Cross uniform, smiling with joy as she walked proudly down the steps to meet her husband, the great victor.

A Private Line

1945–77

At any other time, Clementine would have relished the palatial appointments of an elegant penthouse at Claridge's, her favourite London hotel. But, having been turfed out of Downing Street by an ungrateful electorate, she and Winston simply had nowhere else to go.

Clementine suffered various bouts of ill health after the war. Here she is in April 1950 at the age of 65.

Winston had called a general election a fortnight after VE Day, Beaverbrook predicting he would be voted back to power with a hundred-seat majority. Clementine had been doubtful from the off. Having dealt with her mailbag during the war and toured the country listening to people's woes, she had known that there was a yearning among the populace for social reform and that many saw Labour as the only party to offer credible policies on housing, jobs and social security. Yet, rather than painting a rival vision of a fairer Britain, Winston had opened his campaign with the absurd warning that a Labour government would result in tyranny enforced by a homegrown 'Gestapo'. Clementine had begged him to drop the words from his speech, but it was as if Winston's reason had deserted him.

Neither had Winston been physically fit for the election. During the campaign, he had finally returned to his Woodford constituency, but as he was touring the streets Clementine had realised he was on the point of collapse and had to rush him into a church to rest. Now she often campaigned successfully without him, addressing six hustings on the eve of polling day alone while he travelled up and down the country. The aloof pre-war Clementine with her distinctive glare had been transformed into a formidable and skilled politician.

Polling day had been set for 5 July but the results were delayed for three weeks to allow for the arrival of postal votes from troops overseas. By the time Clementine arrived in Woodford to attend the count, on the morning of the 26th, Winston's only opponent had already amassed surprisingly large piles of votes. As news began to come in that Labour was taking Tory seats by the dozen, Clementine deserted her post and fled back to the Annexe to find Winston staring blankly at the wall of the Map Room, where the results were being posted on a special chart. His seat was safe but every minute brought word of fresh reverses elsewhere.[1] At six o'clock that evening, he ordered drinks and cigars for the staff and set off to Buckingham Palace to resign.

Shock at the election result was felt around the world. From Potsdam, the British ambassador to the USSR, Sir Archibald Clark Kerr, reported to Clementine that the Russian delegation was left 'gibbering and bewildered' at the news. Molotov, whom she had got to know well in Moscow, was 'grey in the face and clearly much upset, throwing up his fat hands and asking why? Why?'[2] Pamela added: 'Poor Clemmie I feel very deeply for her.'

Clementine arrives at a polling station in London during the fateful election of 1945.

Winston Churchill campaigning with his wife Clementine Churchill in his constituency
of Woodford, Essex. Photograph, 26 May 1945.

She was not the only one to worry about Clementine's reaction. Many others, including Clark Kerr, wrote specifically to Clementine to thank her 'for being so uniformly kind'. Winston's chief of staff, General Pug Ismay, wrote emotionally to both of them to say how much their 'kindness' had meant to him. Members of the public sent messages stating how much the 'nation' was in her debt, recognising that Winston could not have achieved 'a quarter' of what he had done without her. In truth, like Winston, Clementine now felt there was little to live for any more – no enemy to overcome, no government to lead, no people to inspire.

Believing Winston lacked the strength to fight on in politics and that his health would soon fail for the last time, Clementine had fervently hoped to persuade him to retire in glory once the war was won. He was seventy years old.

With Chartwell being reconfigured, they instead spent their days brooding in their suite at Claridge's. Having been 'hurled' out of power, as she put it, Clementine found that 'time crawls wearily along'[3] and she pleaded with Mary to return home from her unit in Germany. Clementine blamed herself, 'but I'm finding life more than I can bear' – in large part because Winston was being 'very difficult'. 'I can't see any future,' she told her terrified daughter. 'We are learning how rough & stony the World is.'[4]

When Winston returned in early October from a painting holiday in Italy, their new London house at Hyde Park Gate was ready. The rearrangement of Chartwell was nearly finished, too. But with the Churchills' wartime reprieve now over, even Clementine's economies were not enough to forestall the inevitable financial reckoning and Winston was again forced to consider selling up. It was this prospect that prompted an old friend, Lord Camrose, to marshal other wealthy admirers to buy Chartwell for £50,000 and present it to the National Trust, on condition that Winston and Clementine could go on living there for the rest of their lives.

From helping to run the war Clementine was reduced once more to merely running houses. Feeling redundant and ignored, she longed for Winston to leave politics altogether. But he pursued his own interests in the same self-absorbed way, expecting her to be on tap whenever he needed her for comfort. Late 1945 was marred by bitter rows, and she began to doubt whether he had ever valued her at all. Clementine had continued to attend her Red Cross and other meetings, but now took doctors' advice to cancel her forthcoming engagements. She spent time instead replying to the many

•

The aloof pre-war Clementine with her distinctive glare had been transformed into a formidable and skilled politician.

•

letters of sympathy she received from friends, former staff and members of the public.

Throughout 1946, Winston was festooned with honours from allies and liberated countries around the world. Early in the year, Clementine joined him on a trip to America, where he was showered with honorary degrees and given a civic welcome in New York. In March, he dominated the news with his thunderous speech at Westminster College, Fulton, Missouri, in which he referred to an ominous 'iron curtain' behind which the capitals of Central and Eastern Europe now lay. Although only a year, it seemed a long time since Clementine had been so fêted in Soviet Russia; all her hopes of friendliness between Moscow and the West appeared to have been dashed.

Typically, she hovered in the background as Winston lapped up the attention. She was genuinely surprised if anyone noticed her at all. But in June 1946, two months after her sixty-first birthday and in the last round of honours awarded for wartime achievement, Attlee (now Prime Minister) made her a Dame for her work on the Aid to Russia Fund and the 'many other services which made so marked and brave a contribution'.[5] Other awards were to follow.

It was, however, another two years before she received the recognition that mattered most. On their fortieth wedding anniversary in September 1948, Winston finally put it down in writing. Perhaps only now that others had honoured her did he appreciate how vital she had been during the war. Or maybe because now his own place in history seemed to be sure. In a house note to Clementine, he wrote: 'I send this token, but how little can it express my gratitude to you for making my life & any work I have done possible.'[6]

•

> **Having been 'hurled' out of power, as she put it, Clementine found that 'time crawls wearily along'**

The end of the war had left Clementine with a taste for public duty, but in want of a role. She was therefore pleased in 1949 to be invited to chair the YWCA's National Hostels Committee. It was hardly the United Nations (where Eleanor Roosevelt now held a grand position) but it gave her the chance to exercise her talent for organisation. She soon became an effective scourge of hard mattresses and inadequate bathrooms. Nearly a decade later, she would involve herself in an appeal for World Refugee Year and in

Randolph and Sarah accompany their illustrious parents along the platform of Union Station in Washington DC in March 1946. As the great victor, Winston was showered with honorary degrees across America and received a civic welcome in New York, and also held talks with President Truman.

Above: Clementine received her Insignia of the Dame Grand Cross of the Civil Division of the Order of the British Empire at Buckingham Palace in July 1946 in recognition of her huge contribution to victory in WWII. She was accompanied by her daughters Mary (on the left) and Sarah.

Opposite: The Churchills at Chartwell in 1947. Tea is taken under a large painting of Winston, who is wearing monogrammed slippers. Informal was not Clementine's style.

another for the building of New Hall, Cambridge, the university's third college for women.

While she lacked a prominent public role of her own, she found a new and perhaps unexpected purpose in her grandchildren. In February 1947, Mary married diplomat Christopher Soames. Although Clementine was initially untrusting (and perhaps a little jealous) of this new arrival, over time she grew to like and rely on him. Although never a nappy changer, she doted on the grandchildren who soon followed. Mary recalled how at one family picnic, her mother remarked, 'You have so much fun with your children that I now realise how I missed out.'[7]

Diana and her husband, Duncan Sandys, and their three children, were also frequent visitors to Chartwell. Meanwhile, in rare reflective moments, Randolph was forced to concede how his mother had gone out of her way to help him. As chairwoman of a trust set up at the end of the war to look after Winston's children and grandchildren, she quietly bailed out his heir from his

Clementine and Winston with
the grandchildren at Chartwell
in 1951. Clementine was a kind
but not cosy grandmother.

extravagances. Randolph married again in November 1948, and Clementine bought the newlyweds a house.

Sarah returned to acting after the war and in the autumn of 1946 signed up with an Italian film company in Rome, but happiness eluded her. Having been rejected by her, on 3 November 1947, a distraught Gil Winant took a pistol and shot himself at his home in Concord, New Hampshire. Clementine sent four dozen yellow roses to his funeral and made Winston accompany her to Winant's London memorial service at St Paul's. She was rigid with grief at the loss of her friend; Sarah was riven with guilt.

The next general election, in February 1950, saw Labour returned to power by the narrowest of margins. Despite a minor stroke, growing deafness and a hernia operation, Winston's health appeared surprisingly robust and his attacks on Labour's record were beginning to draw blood. Clementine, too, was feeling better about life, until in May 1951 she was admitted to hospital for a major gynaecological 'repair'. This time she could afford not to stint on her convalescence; she spent weeks resting at Chartwell before embarking on holidays in south-west France, Paris, the Alps and Venice. A snap election was called on her return in early October and the Tories came home with a majority of seventeen seats. Just short of his seventy-seventh birthday, Winston was once again Prime Minister.

Of course there was satisfaction that he had been restored to power after the ignominy of 1945, but she thought him too old and his health too compromised for high office. Being in the thick of things again no doubt offered some compensation, though. Winston consulted her, as usual, on

The Churchills attend the christening of their grandchild Charlotte Soames at the local Westerham parish church in November 1954. With them are the baby's elder siblings, Nicholas (now an MP), Emma and Jeremy Soames.

Opposite: Clementine became a warm and accomplished speaker able to work the crowd with aplomb. Although never a true Tory here she is addressing the Conservative party conference at Earl's Court, London, in 1949.

Above: The Churchills, shown here at Epsom racecourse to watch the Derby in 1949, enjoyed a similar sense of humour. Her laugh, however, was much louder than his.

Clementine and Winston arrive at St Paul's Cathedral in London in October 1951 for a service before the forthcoming general election.

appointments – including his plan to offer the prestigious role of War Secretary to Duncan Sandys. She quickly warned that he would be exposing himself to allegations of nepotism and Sandys was duly downgraded to the more junior post of Minister of Supply. This intervention aside, however, Clementine struggled to summon her old enthusiasm for government. The mould she had broken in 1940, becoming Britain's first First Lady, contracted back into a more conventional (and perhaps constitutionally correct) shape during Winston's second term. She involved herself more with hospitality and ceremony than in helping to run the country. She returned to a 10 Downing

Street that had physically changed since her previous residency. Clementine knew better than to spend public money on a lavish redecoration, but she somehow worked wonders on the fine Georgian rooms. The Bristol glass chandeliers were scrubbed to sparkling perfection and the addition of simple bunches of flowers, family photographs and William Nicholson paintings in muted colours, displayed in bevelled frames, banished the austerity-era dreariness.[8]

George VI died on 6 February 1952. A couple of weeks later, Winston suffered from a spasm of the cerebral arteries that caused temporary confusion in his speech. The condition was kept secret outside a small inner circle but it raised questions about how long he could carry on. At the same time, Clementine was also weakening. Suffering from an overwhelming sensation of fatigue, she cancelled her public engagements that summer and resorted to her old pattern of taking 'cures'.

•

Large-scale entertaining, however, became the dominant chore of Clementine's second life at Number 10, particularly in the prelude to the coronation of Queen Elizabeth II on 2 June 1953. There was a succession of state visits, a Commonwealth Conference, a banquet for the heads of state and government attending the coronation, and a whirl of other lunches, dinners and receptions. On the great day, Clementine draped herself in the satin robe of the Order of the British Empire and borrowed a tiara from a friend. Riding beside Winston in a coach during the procession she looked radiant, but the strain of the preparations had taken its toll. Though barely noticeable, her arm was encased in a sling because of neuritis, a painful inflammation of the nerves that would in time drive her once again to near-collapse.

Three weeks later, Clementine hosted a dinner for thirty-eight at Downing Street in honour of the Italian Prime Minister, Alcide De Gasperi. As the guests were leaving the first-floor Pillared Room, she glanced back to see Winston struggling to rise from his chair. Christopher Soames quickly informed De Gasperi that the Prime Minister was over-tired, and others present apparently attributed the slur in his speech to the wine. It was

> For once Randolph marvelled at his mother's capacity to deal with a crisis – she had herself broken several ribs in a fall

confirmed in the morning that he had suffered another stroke, although – incredibly – he still held Cabinet, at which his colleagues noticed little untoward. The following day, however, he was much worse and had to be bundled out of town to the seclusion of Chartwell.

Moran feared Winston would not last the weekend and the family swiftly gathered around him. For once Randolph marvelled at his mother's capacity to deal with a crisis – she had herself broken several ribs in a fall. With Winston still far from capable of running the country, unavoidable decisions were being taken by Colville and Soames on the basis of what they thought he would have done, and it is more than probable – for she was in constant attendance – that they did so after consultation with Clementine. Such was the blanket secrecy about his condition and the small, makeshift (and undemocratic) band running the country that only carefully selected visitors were permitted. These the ever-alert Clementine waylaid beforehand, making them promise not to offer him unrealistic hopes of staying at Number 10.

As Winston gradually recuperated, so did his impatience rapidly increase. The Churchills argued bitterly over whether he should accept an invitation from the Queen to go horse racing in September and then stay with her at Balmoral. True to form, Winston quickly apologised for losing his temper, although he also got his way. Perhaps Clementine had been unreasonably pessimistic: after the strain of the past couple of months, Balmoral proved to be an uplifting break.

After Winston resumed his full duties as Prime Minister in October 1953, a disapproving Clementine fled from him yet again. Although he was stronger, he found her absence troubling. Even news that he had won the Nobel Prize for Literature failed to lift his mood. In any case, he was prevented from receiving the award in person by having to attend a summit with President Eisenhower. Clementine flew to Stockholm in his place; here she was welcomed not as a mere substitute for her husband, but as an honoured guest in her own right.

She was becoming increasingly 'aggressive' with Winston, however, refusing to accept his failing health as an excuse for rudeness. When on one occasion he slumped in a chair, yawned widely and made no effort to talk to a visiting relative, Clementine rebuked him by administering a sharp tap on the knuckles with a fork.[9] Her mood was not eased by her neuritis. The treatment favoured by her doctors – and by Clementine herself – seems as before to have been to escape from Downing Street, and so in

May she packed her bags for a three-week 'cure' at Aix-les-Bains in south-eastern France.

Even without neuritis, she would have had reason to seek solace. Sadness tinged virtually every aspect of Clementine's life in the 1950s. Devastated by her husband's flamboyant womanising, Diana had suffered a nervous breakdown around the same time as Winston's stroke. Clementine was dismayed to see her daughter in such agony, but their relationship had never been strong and at this point it appears to have collapsed altogether.

Sarah tried to help, but her own marriage to photographer Antony Beauchamp was in trouble. By August 1957, she was on the brink of filing for divorce when Clementine phoned her with tragic news: Antony had taken his life by an overdose of sleeping pills. Yet again a man Sarah had loved had

An upbeat campaign returned Winston to power in October 1951, and Clementine stands next to him as he gives the 'V' sign from the window of Conservative headquarters in his constituency.

committed suicide – and all the self-recrimination that had attended Gil Winant's death came flooding back. In January 1958, she was arrested outside her Malibu Beach home and charged with drunkenness.

Clementine quickly arranged for Sarah to fly out to the south of France away from the press pack. She joined her for a few days, and during her long, non-judgemental talks with her daughter, the two women drew much closer.

Clementine herself had few confidantes to turn to, for she had also lost her sole surviving sibling to cancer. Nellie died, aged sixty-six, in February 1955, little more than six months after her diagnosis. One of Nellie's last outings had been to Winston's eightieth birthday party in November 1954, which had itself not been the joyful occasion Clementine would have wished. Parliament had decided to mark the occasion by presenting him with a portrait by the fashionable artist Graham Sutherland. When they saw the finished work, Clementine was initially intrigued by the treatment, but Winston's reaction was one of instant loathing – and she, too, came to resent how it presented an ancient, grumpy figure in depressing greys and browns.

The 23,000 birthday telegrams and cards that poured in from around the world helped to lift both their spirits so that by 30 November itself, they were able to receive the painting in good grace. As Parliament welcomed them in Westminster Hall with a deafening ovation, Clementine glowed. Afterwards the portrait was hidden away in the basement at Chartwell, until, one day, Clementine asked her secretary, Grace, for her help. Grace offered to destroy it and, with the help of her brother, sneaked it out of Chartwell 'in the dead of night' and took it by van to his home several miles away, where they lit a bonfire in the back garden. She threw the painting on the fire and watched it burn, telling Clementine the next morning what she had done.

The birthday applause had been genuine, but so were the growing concerns about Winston's 'twilight' powers. One morning in July 1954, Harold Macmillan, then Minister of Housing, visited Clementine alone in Downing Street. He told her Winston no longer commanded the support of all his Cabinet colleagues, and would have to step down. She listened and agreed to convey his arguments to her husband.[10] When she finally summoned up the resolve to relate the morning's events, Winston reacted surprisingly well, merely summoning Macmillan that afternoon to inform him that he intended to 'soldier on'. Clementine never forgave the man she now considered the leader of an anti-Winston cabal, but this time her husband's majestic career was really at an end.

Above: Clementine gives a speech after
she accepted the Nobel Prize for Literature
on Winston's behalf in Stockholm on
10 December 1953.

Opposite: Clementine charms King Gustaf VI
Adolf of Sweden at the Nobel Banquet. Queen
Louise of Sweden described her honoured
guest's presence as nothing short of 'queenly'.

The Churchills at home at Hyde Park Gate on the occasion of Winston's 85th birthday. By now his failing health required the attention of a male nurse as well as Clementine's ever-solicitous eye.

First, however, they held one of their famously good parties. The invitation cards had stated merely that Sir Winston was 'At Home' to celebrate Lady Churchill's seventieth birthday, yet there were distinct undertones that the event also marked the end of an era. Clementine's Labour friends were present among the convivial crowd and she made a point of greeting Mrs Attlee with a kiss. Cecil Beaton heard that she was in agony (she confessed to Violet Asquith that she was 'doped' up to ensure she was 'gay as a lark'), but he also noted that there was still 'fire and dash in the consort of the old warrior'.

With the newspapers on strike, the reaction was surprisingly muted when Winston resigned a few days later on the afternoon of 5 April 1955. The following day, the Churchills hosted a goodbye tea party for the Downing Street staff and Winston departed for Chartwell, cheers ringing in his ears as he walked the long corridor from the Cabinet Room to the front door for the last time.

So began the Churchills' final stretch outside the magic circle of power – and with no hope of rejoining it, Winston descended into a 'state of apathy and indifference'.[12] Nevertheless, Clementine's daughters agreed that the adjustment to private life was worse for her than for Winston. He was still showered with admiring attention, had his cronies, his painting and writing and, above all, Chartwell. By contrast, Clementine had hoped to enjoy their liberation from high office by socialising in London and going to the theatre. But decades of devotion to Winston had left her with few friends, and Nellie's death had robbed her of one of her few remaining sources of female companionship. Mostly, in her loneliness, she turned to the young women she employed as secretaries. She took them to the royal box at Wimbledon, to the theatre, cinema and art galleries, and invited them for lunch, drinks or even just to watch television.

Clementine returned to Chartwell from a visit to St Moritz in September 1955 in good spirits, only for her neuritis to flare up again within a couple of months. A Chartwell family Christmas saw a brief improvement in her condition, but in January 1956 she was admitted to hospital for three weeks. Winston had already returned to the south of France. He wrote to her every couple of days and at one point planned to return. Clementine preferred him to stay put and, upon finally being discharged, ignored his entreaties to convalesce with him and set off instead on an eight-week cruise to Ceylon (modern-day Sri Lanka). She returned to Britain in better humour on

So began the Churchills' final stretch outside the magic circle of power – and with no hope of rejoining it, Winston descended into a 'state of apathy and indifference'.

The birthday applause had been genuine, but so were the
growing concerns about Winston's 'twilight' powers.

Opposite: The Queen and Prince Philip are greeted by Winston and Clementine for a dinner party
at Downing Street in 1955, shortly before he stepped down as Prime Minister.

Above: A family photograph from 1955. Front row from left to right: Clementine, Lady Eden (née Clarissa
Churchill, Winston's niece and wife of incoming PM Anthony Eden), Mary and Sarah.
Diana is second from the right at the back, with Winston in the centre.

So began the
Churchills' final stretch
outside the magic
circle of power.

•

12 April but departed after only a month for Paris. In August, she again journeyed to St Moritz. The Churchills had re-established a mutually viable pattern: short periods together in London or Chartwell, between often lengthy trips apart.

At the end of September 1958, Winston and Clementine were invited to join a Mediterranean cruise on Aristotle Onassis' yacht, the *Christina*. They boarded on a high, having just celebrated their golden wedding anniversary together at La Capponcina, Lord Beaverbrook's villa near Monte Carlo. But inevitably, not even the most luxurious existence could protect the Churchills from the depredations of old age. Since mid-1958, Winston had employed a male nurse, and as he entered his late eighties he began to suffer from further bouts of pneumonia. Especially troubling was his descent into deafness. Clementine badgered him to wear a hearing aid, but he resisted what he felt to be a fiddly imposition: he talked less and less, leaving her to fill the lulls in conversation. So far as she was able, she tried to keep his chin up, but Clementine was now carrying the burden of a husband who openly wanted to die.

Nor was she in fine fettle herself. After at last conquering her neuritis in the summer of 1958, she had developed shingles. Recurrent flu dogged her winters, while she continued to suffer from periodic lows. In 1961, she agreed to be admitted to hospital for a complete rest and check-up. There was no obvious physical cause of her severe fatigue but she was formally diagnosed with depression.

After Winston's resignation as Prime Minister, Clementine was obliged once again to act as his proxy in his constituency. Nevertheless, in the election year of 1959, he returned to Woodford to make it clear he would be standing again. So, that October, at the age of seventy-four, Clementine joined Winston on the trail to fight their fifteenth election together. Weary as she was, she understood that this remnant of a once magnificent public life was virtually the last stimulus left to her husband.

Three years later, in the summer of 1962, Winston broke his hip in a fall. Clementine rarely felt able to leave his side as he was an obstreperous patient and a danger to himself when left unattended. Now virtually unable to walk, he wanted merely to sit silently gazing into the fire or, when at Chartwell, at the view. Even mealtimes passed with barely a flicker of the old Winston; Clementine had to shout to make herself heard. Sometimes he lay in bed all day doing nothing. He told Diana, 'My life is over, but not yet ended.'[13]

Clementine, a lifelong art lover, encouraged her husband to paint but preferred looking at art herself. Here she is attending a record-setting auction in London in 1958 in which works by Cézanne, Manet, van Gogh and Renoir were sold.

Randolph and his daughter Arabella join Clementine and Winston in the south of
France for their golden wedding anniversary in September 1958.

Finally, in May 1963, Winston accepted the realities of his own position. With great sadness, he announced he would not be standing again as an MP; he was eighty-nine. The Commons prepared to pay him a special tribute. But when Clementine received a copy of the proposed wording the following year, ever his protector-in-chief, she reacted with cold fury, denouncing it as 'mangy'.[14] It was duly rewritten to her liking to include a reference to the House's 'unbounded admiration and gratitude' for Winston's services to the nation and the world and, above all, his 'inspiration of the British people when they stood alone'. She was at his side when the resolution was delivered by a delegation led by the Prime Minister, Sir Alec Douglas-Home.

Although Winston's health appeared to rally over the summer, by the autumn of 1963 it was clear that Clementine's was deteriorating. She became so overwrought that in early October she had to be sedated and admitted to Westminster Hospital, where her severe depression was treated with electro-convulsive therapy (ECT). She was still in hospital when, during the night of 19–20 October, Diana, who had also been receiving ECT,[15] took a huge overdose of sleeping pills and was found dead on the bedroom floor of her Belgravia flat. Her death was both 'unexpected' and 'inexplicable'. Mary had to rush to the hospital, while still reeling from the shock, to break the news to her mother before she heard it on the radio. One small mercy was that Clementine was already heavily sedated, cushioning the blow. Clementine was released from hospital only the day before Diana's funeral and neither she nor Winston was well enough to attend – although they were both present at the memorial service the following week. An air of immeasurable sadness now hung over the Churchill family.

•

After Winston's resignation as Prime Minister, Clementine was obliged once again to act as his proxy in his constituency.

•

In November 1964, when Winston turned ninety, Clementine took great care over his birthday celebrations, beginning by singing him 'Happy Birthday' in his bedroom in the morning. Later she gathered the clan for a candlelit feast of all his favourite dishes. He beamed at everyone, but was obviously frail and somehow detached. In the New Year, on 12 January, he suffered another stroke, and over the following days slid into a coma. Clementine brought in a priest to pray at his bedside, but mostly she sat serenely, holding his right

hand, his beloved marmalade cat asleep at his feet. He was deeply unconscious, but clasped her fingers so tightly the nurses were convinced he was aware of her presence. Slipping quietly into his bedroom, the family came to see these two great figures together for one last time. Winston took his final breaths on the cold winter morning of 24 January.

Two days afterwards, his body was taken to Westminster Hall to lie in state until burial on 30 January. Every day, often after dark, Clementine slipped in through a side door to watch the mournful but dignified queues of people coming to pay their last respects.

Winston had long ago declared that he wanted to be buried like a soldier. Clementine was consulted to ensure that his wishes were carried out (he wanted military bands, for instance, of which he was given nine), but in any case the Queen had previously made it clear that he would be granted the honour of a full state funeral. Thus, with imperial ceremony, Winston's coffin was drawn slowly through London's streets from Westminster to St Paul's Cathedral. Hundreds of thousands lined the route. Clementine, with Sarah and Mary, followed in silence in the Queen's horse-drawn coach, equipped with lap rugs and hot-water bottles against the penetrating chill. Randolph lent his arm to his mother and escorted her inside, where fifteen present and past heads of state, including Presidents de Gaulle and Eisenhower, were among the thousands waiting. Another mourner, Cecil Beaton, thought age and grief made Clementine look more beautiful than ever. He found himself unutterably moved by 'the face of Lady Churchill asking for instructions as to procedure, with small jerky little steps, yet marvellously dignified, a face in a crowd, another sample of selflessness and pure feeling'.[16] Yet she still frowned upon 'crying on parade', and remained dry-eyed all through the day.

At the brief private burial at Bladon, the Blenheim parish church, with just the family and a few close friends around her, Clementine laid a wreath of roses, tulips and carnations, and bade her private farewell with the words: 'I will soon be with you again.'[17]

•

Clementine never spent another night at Chartwell. Not that her devotion to Winston diminished; henceforth, her work became guarding his reputation

Opposite: The Churchills arrive home at Hyde Park Gate in 1959 after a trip to the US to see President Eisenhower.

•

Although Winston's health appeared to rally over the summer, by the autumn of 1963 it was clear that Clementine's was deteriorating.

•

At her desk at Hyde Park Gate, on the occasion of Clementine's 78th birthday in 1963. She always favoured natural arrangements of garden flowers.

instead. To that end, she handed the house over to the National Trust and asked for it to be returned to the appearance and layout of its 1930s' heyday; Winston was to be remembered as a great statesman and warrior rather than a mere frail human being.

Home for Clementine was now an elegant London flat a stone's throw from Hyde Park. Diana's daughter, Celia Sandys, visited often and remembers that her grandmother continued to live in considerable style. Clementine had drawn Celia closer to her since Diana's suicide in 1963. After Winston's death she also softened her attitude to Randolph, and mother and son at last found some enjoyment in each other.

Four months after Winston's funeral, the Labour Prime Minister Harold Wilson made Clementine a life peer as Baroness Spencer-Churchill of Chartwell. She was thrilled at entering Parliament on her own account and derived great pleasure from taking her seat in the House of Lords on the crossbenches. That first year she made thirteen appearances, but in 1966 she attended just seven times and she did not vote nor make a speech. In the past she had shown considerable flair for politics, but at the age of eighty, with her hearing and sight fading, her body if not her mind was no longer up to the task.

There was, however, release. An almost ethereal calm seems to have descended on Clementine during her nearly thirteen years as a widow. All those nervous complaints largely disappeared, even if the harsh challenges of her life did not. The sudden if not entirely unexpected death of Randolph from a heart attack at the age of fifty-seven in June 1968 hit her cruelly of course, but there was no emotional collapse as of old, merely a controlled silence.

Clementine enjoyed the winter of her life as she had always hoped: living in London and visiting theatres and galleries. As Winston's former secretary, Jane Portal, put it: 'Perhaps at the end she was, while treasuring her memories, able finally to be herself.' On good days she was still capable of tilting her head back to emit a youthful-sounding laugh. Clementine could surely be forgiven for feeling a sense of relief immediately after Winston's death; no doubt her existence without him was more restful, and life had merely clung to him in his final years. But as she grew older, his absence pained her more and more.

The end came on 12 December 1977. Immaculately dressed as always, Clementine was lunching at home when her new secretary, Nonie Chapman,

Still cutting a dash at nearly 75, here Clementine sports her favourite sunglasses on a trip
with Winston to Monte Carlo in July 1959.

Randolph followed his father's coffin with his mother on his arm. She remained upright and dry-eyed throughout the funeral on 30 January 1965 and ordered the rest of the family to do the same.

Clementine laid this note on Winston's grave with a funeral wreath of roses, tulips and carnations. 31 January 1965.

Finally a Parliamentarian in her own right. Six months after Winston's death,
Clementine is introduced to the House of Lords as Baroness Spencer, Churchill
of Chartwell. She took her place on the crossbenches.

noticed a sudden change in her breathing. She died a few minutes later
from a heart attack, aged ninety-two, proud and unbowed until the end.
Her funeral, attended only by family and close friends, was held a few
days afterwards at Holy Trinity, Brompton, where she had worshipped
in her latter years. She was buried quietly with Winston at Bladon, as she
had always planned.

On 24 January 1978, thirteen years to the day after Winston's death,
a memorial service was held for Clementine at Westminster Abbey. The
Labour Prime Minister James Callaghan attended, as did the leaders of
the Conservative and Liberal parties, Margaret Thatcher and David Steel.
Her grandson, Winston, read an extract from the sermon spoken at her
wedding, including the prescient lines: 'There must be in the statesman's
life many times when he depends upon the love, the insight, the penetrating
sympathy and devotion of his wife.'

It should never be forgotten how Clementine overcame prejudice, even
ridicule, to do much that a woman had never done before. Although she had
no political status of her own, Winston's unfailing trust in and dependence on
her meant that she was able to command civil servants, dress down generals,
chivvy Cabinet ministers and face up to presidents on his behalf. Her power
and influence – and the results she achieved – would be unthinkable for a
prime ministerial spouse today.

She had her faults, not least her shortcomings as a mother. But Clementine
was the lodestar for one of the greatest men of the twentieth century and he
loved her without question for nearly sixty years. Ultimately, Winston
recognised that his greatest achievements would have eluded him but for his
wife's unflinching belief and guidance. She boosted and never betrayed him;
she counselled but also challenged; she chided as well as consoled. She
shored up his inadequacies, moderated his extremes and stopped him making
countless mistakes. Without her by his side, sharing the burden, it is difficult,
if not impossible to imagine him leading Britain, against almost impossible
odds, to victory over tyranny. As she inspired and sustained Winston, so
did she help lead her country through its darkest hour. When, in 1940,
he became Prime Minister of a country fighting for its survival, Winston
declared he had nothing to offer but blood, toil, tears and sweat. In truth,
he should have added to this now legendary list.

Last, but not least, he had Clemmie.

> It should never
> be forgotten how
> Clementine overcame
> prejudice, even ridicule,
> to do much that a
> woman had never
> done before.

Clementine was the lodestar for one of the greatest men of the twentieth century and he loved her without question for nearly sixty years. Ultimately, Winston recognised that his greatest achievements would have eluded him but for his wife's unflinching belief and guidance.

Pulling power. Clementine could still draw a crowd into old age. Here she is emerging from the Café Royal in London on 1 April 1965, after celebrating her 80th birthday with her family.

EPILOGUE

During her almost thirteen years as his widow, Clementine devoted herself to ensuring her husband's legacy, but perhaps even she would be surprised at the attention and adulation he continues to receive. Since his death in 1965, Winston has become the most biographed figure of all time – and now also one of the most popular figures in Hollywood. In short order, he has held sway over a blockbuster Netflix series, three major movies and a constant flurry of new biographies assessing his life from every angle, from his money to his medicines. The legend of the Brit who stood alone against the Nazis in 1940 has aged well; its potency in this century as remarkable as ever.

Yet for all the fervour for Winston's continuing ability to intrigue and inspire, it is the evolving portrayal of Clementine that has truly captured the imagination most recently. Slowly but surely, she has emerged from the shadows to assume her rightful place in history as his closest counsel and the chief architect of Churchill's greatness. Now, finally, screenwriters and others have showcased the popular power of a style icon who ventured far beyond the traditional feminine sphere to have enormous and lasting historical impact. It has become clear to many that without Clementine taking her rightful place, only part of the epic Churchill story has hitherto been told. It seems certain that Clementine, who never sought glory on her own account, would have been astonished at the way in which her public profile is now increasing by the day.

Letters, official papers, first-person testimony and memoirs reveal how Clementine evolved into becoming Britain's first First Lady; she is still probably the only figure to have fulfilled that challenging and pivotal role.

Opposite: Clementine in her dotage: a portrait by Godfrey Argent taken in 1967, two years after Winston's death.

The fact that she did so when the nation was engaged in a death battle for survival compelled Clementine to play a part she invented from scratch, but which ultimately led her to command civil servants, dress down generals, chivvy cabinet ministers and face up to presidents on Winston's behalf.

The publication, in 2015, of the first edition of the unabridged version of this book sought to draw attention to not just how crucial Clementine had been to her husband's career, but also to Allied victory in the Second World War: to how Churchill was not some emotional island devoid of need, but (according to his doctor) a man who drew on his wife's resolve to shore up his own strength; and how the wartime chief of staff, Pug Ismay, observed that the history of Winston Churchill and the history of the world would have been quite different without Clementine's unflinching interventions and belief. As Clement Attlee put it, the way she managed a character he considered 'half-genius, half-bloody fool' to achieve his rightful status as global legend, was in itself a type of genius. Certainly, Clementine could not have invested more in her partnership with Winston, one that was almost certainly the most important of its time. Now there is an appetite for that contribution to be portrayed more fairly: for Clementine's story of triumph over adversity, prejudice, ill health and even ridicule in order to help shape monumental global events, to be acknowledged and understood. Previous biographies of Churchill, written in a different age and which fail to give her a single mention, perhaps now look regressive and certainly incomplete.

The Great Man view of history – subscribed to by Winston himself, unsurprisingly – has always tended to ignore or devalue the significance of marriage. Or, indeed, the role of any other than the Great Man himself. But the very qualities that made Winston a supreme statesman – a sense of destiny combined with a blinkered drive and focus – were also sometimes his undoing. It is fair to say that without a countervailing force in his life, one able and prepared to stand up to him when necessary, he would probably have been wrecked by them. Clementine married a man variously described as 'the largest human being of our times' and 'the stuff of which tyrants are made'. That he never became one was in no small part down to his wife. Clementine fulfilled that many-faceted role throughout the Churchills' six decades together, but most of all when Winston was Prime Minister during the war.

Books such as this one aim to reveal the full story; sometimes then cinema picks up the baton. Two actresses have done much to convey some of Clementine's true stature on the screen. Both Kristin Scott Thomas, the actress who played Clementine in *Darkest Hour* (2017), and Harriet Walter, who took the role in the Netflix series *The Crown* (2016–2019) fought hard to beef up their parts in recognition of their character's little-understood role in Churchill's and the nation's life story. They had both researched Clementine's life and so knew that she deserved a proper outing for twenty-first century audiences, more eager than ever before to give women in history their proper due. And yet, as with so many biographies and films before them, neither production initially gave more than a passing nod to Clementine's political as well as her emotional acumen. Indeed, Scott Thomas turned down the part until Clementine's part was made more 'pro-active'. 'Give her more of a motor,' she told director Joe Wright, 'and then I might want to do it.' It is testament to the actress's cinematic status that her request was granted – at least to some extent.

Thanks in part to these actresses' efforts, Clementine's extraordinary importance is finally beginning to shine through beyond these pages. No longer is she widely viewed through the prism of mere cipher, but as a considerable figure in her own right. Audiences and the media have consequently become intrigued with her and started to demand more – Scott Thomas has been particularly vocal about the need for a screen biopic devoted to Clementine's exceptional story. The hope and expectation now must be that Clementine will finally be granted her moment of glory on the big screen; a treatment in which she takes her place at the centre of events.

We have come a long way from the time not that long ago when many younger British adults were not even aware that Churchill had a wife, and almost all would have been unable to identify her in a picture. Certainly, few, if any, knew that Clementine was the surprising product of a promiscuous mother, a broken home and a suburban grammar school education – or that she was related to Britain's most newsworthy aristocratic family – the Mitfords.

Yet there are people who have treasured memories of Clementine, who sensed that we only know a quarter of what she actually achieved. Several older readers from across the world have contacted me to share their memories of her – whether drawing on letters of encouragement, written to them by Clementine when they were children during the war, or about how they used to call coats with a fastening at the throat 'Clementines' in tribute to her 'look'.

Some had moving personal stories to tell, including one particularly distressing account from a member of the audience at a literary festival who had been a nurse on the London hospital ward where Clementine was being treated for depression in 1963, when news came through of her daughter Diana's suicide. The most junior member of the nursing team, she recounted how such were the fears about Clementine's reaction that one of her duties had been to ensure there were padlocks on all the windows. This woman had been carrying the memory of Clementine for nearly sixty years, her sympathy and soaring admiration for her eminent, but distraught patient, undimmed during that time. It is a poignant reminder that great people can suffer terribly, too.

Despite her evident troubles, Clementine left a legacy – of inspiration and hope – more lasting and universal to those who met her or whose lives were touched by her. Take photographer Cecil Beaton's account of a party in April 1955, held shortly before Churchill's final departure from Downing Street, when he found himself fixated by seventy-year-old Clementine's 'Grecian profile, the deep-set pale blue eyes' and by the fact that even at that age, he detected 'fire and dash in the consort of the old warrior'.[11] What is fascinating is the strength of the impression that Clementine made during her lifetime – and how that almost completely faded from view for nigh on half a century after her death, until now.

Of course, there have since been many first ladies who have left their mark – notably in the United States where, unlike the Prime Minister's consort in Britain, the wife of the president enjoys a quasi-constitutional status. Jackie Kennedy's sleek shift dresses and pillbox hats of the 1960s set a whole new vogue across the globe – but she never came close to Clementine's political force. Hillary Clinton was deeply involved in her husband Bill's administration in the 1990s, but never managed to win the emotional support of the majority of Americans. Nor did Cherie Blair, in Britain, win mass popular approval; her status as a clever, opinionated wife to Tony and prominent barrister was rewarded by a constant and unkind portrayal in the press. History will also judge – perhaps harshly – Brigitte Macron after reports of her being overheard loudly admonishing her husband, the President of France, for making too many mistakes.

Perhaps all occupants of the first lady role have struggled – including the early Michelle Obama – to strike the right balance between making the most of their public platform and not overstepping what is perceived as expectable or permissible. Or to intervene without being seen to do so or, even worse, inadvertently undermine the very figure they seek to boost. Clementine seems to have been particularly adept at keeping to that perilous tightrope and avoiding public comment – although in the pre-mass and social media age that would have been much easier.

Clementine's elegance merely enhanced her political nous – she adeptly exploited it to further her husband's ambitions – and perhaps made speaking her mind a little easier. No wonder, that the George W. Bush Presidential Center featured Clementine prominently in its First Ladies Initiative of 2017, believing she could provide an almost unique brand of example and guidance for future consorts of world leaders in our challenging and uncertain times. I was delighted to be involved.

Yet privileging the nation's interests over her own or her family's wellbeing came at a terrible price. In her search for perfection, Clementine succumbed to several bouts of severe and terrifying depression, as witnessed above by the young nurse in 1963. Clementine's record of mothering her children was clearly imperfect, and arguably led to much unhappiness – but then Winston was hardly any better as a consistent or attentive father. Clementine saw it as her principal duty and life's work to prove herself worthy of her exceptional husband and, in 1914 and 1939 when the First and Second World Wars erupted, to help him win those wars. All else was sacrificed on that altar, whatever the personal cost.

The dividend was that she became the driving force behind one of the greatest men of the twentieth century. Winston claimed marrying her had been his most brilliant achievement and stated that none of his life's work would have been possible without her. She was in a way his ultimate authority, his conscience and the nearest he had to a direct line to the people – which was helped by Clementine growing up well outside the Churchillian gilded circle of aristocratic privilege, including in the fish market of Dieppe.

Clementine's glamour propped up Winston's public image when his career hit the buffers (as it frequently did); her empathy for other people smoothed the feathers he had ruffled (which happened all too often); her glittering hospitality disarmed enemies, united allies and enabled her husband to operate from a position of strength and security. Thus, the question is no longer what Clementine did for her husband, but rather how much Winston Churchill could have achieved without her.

FOOTNOTES

INTRODUCTION

[1] Oliver Pawle, *The War and Colonel Warden*, p302.
In the end, there were around 4000 British, American and Canadian deaths on D-Day itself.

[2] Lord Moran, *The Struggle for Survival*, p244

[3] Violet Bonham Carter, *Winston Churchill As I Knew Him*, p18

[4] Elizabeth Nel, *Mr Churchill's Secretary*, p187

[5] CSCT, 10 August 1921

[6] CSCT, 6 August 1928

[7] In fact they were pale blue.

[8] It was a dark reddish-gold, turning to silver in middle age.

[9] Cherie Blair and Cate Haste, *The Goldfish Bowl: Married to the Prime Minister*, p15

[10] Kenneth Harris, *Attlee*, p412

[11] Diana Farr, *Five at Ten*, pp104–5, quoted by Blair and Haste, p121

[12] Blair, *Goldfish Bowl*, p263

[13] Gil Winant, *A Letter from Grosvenor Square*, p46

CHAPTER ONE
The Level of Events

[1] Clementine Spencer Churchill Trust papers (CSCT), notes for My Early Life

[2] Winston Churchill, *My Early Life*

[3] Arthur Lee, *A Good Innings*, p97

[4] CSCT 2/1

[5] Ibid.

[6] Former secretary Nonie Chapman, recorded in Churchill Oral History Archives 3

CHAPTER TWO
More Than Meets the Eye

[1] Asquith Papers, MS Bonham Carter 153

[2] Martin Gilbert, *Winston S. Churchill* Vol. IV, pp. 893–4

[3] MS Bonham Carter 165

[4] CSCT, 12 September 1909

[5] CSCT, 14 July 1912

[6] CSCT, 18 April 1912

[7] CSCT 1/8

[8] I am grateful for this summary from Michael Shelden in *Young Titan*

CHAPTER THREE
The Pain and the Pride

[1] CSCT, 14 August 1914

[2] Gilbert, *Winston S. Churchill* vol. III, pp824–5

[3] Sally Bedell Smith, *Reflected Glory: The Life of Pamela Harriman*, p67

[4] 26 February 1915, H. H. Asquith, *Letters to Venetia Stanley*, p450

[5] Jack Fishman, *My Darling Clementine*, p57

[6] Shelden, *Young Titan*, p321

CHAPTER FOUR
I Believe in Your Star

[1] CSCT, 21 November 1915

[2] CSCT, 19 November 1915

[3] CSCT, 28 December 1915

[4] Chartwell Papers, Winston S. Churchill collection (CHAR), 27 February 1916

[5] CHAR, 13 March 1916

[6] CHAR, 6 April 1916

CHAPTER FIVE
Loss Unimaginable

[1] CSCT, 14 September 1919

[2] Walter H. Thompson, *Assignment: Churchill*, p7

CHAPER SIX
A Chandelier's Life and Sparkle

[1] Author's interview with Lady Williams, née Jane Portal

[2] Mary Soames, *Clementine Churchill*, p97

[3] CHAR, 28 January 1922

[4] Soames, *Clementine Churchill*, p238

[5] Cita Stelzer, *Dinner with Churchill*, p159

[6] Soames, *Clementine Churchill*, p266

CHAPTER SEVEN
Temptation and Redemption

[1] Mary Soames (ed.), *Speaking for Themselves*, p277

[2] Ashley Jackson, *Churchill*, p217

[3] Author's interview with John Julius Norwich

[4] CSCT, 17 February 1931

[5] Soames, *Clementine Churchill*, p275

6   CSCT, 21 February 1936

7   John Pearson, *Citadel of the Heart*, p271

8   Pearson, *Citadel of the Heart*, p213

9   Geoffrey Best, *Churchill: A Study in Greatness*, p150

10 CHAR, 13 December 1938

11 CSCT, 27 July 1939

CHAPTER EIGHT

World of Accident and Storm

1   Duff Cooper, *Diaries*, p275

2   Thompson, *Assignment*, p127

3   Soames, *Clementine Churchill*, p316

4   Diana Cooper, *Trumpets from the Steep*, p38

5   Pamela Harriman Papers (PHP), Box 4

6   Ibid., p243

7   Cowles, *The Era and the Man*, p318

8   John Colville, *Fringes of Power*, p281

9   Sir John Wheeler-Bennet (ed.), *Action This Day*, p140

10 PHP Box 3

11 Fishman, *My Darling Clementine*, p147

12 Moran, *Struggle for Survival*, p15

13 Fishman, *My Darling Clementine*, p154

14 PHP Box 3

15 Winston Churchill, *Second World War*, Vol II, p226

16 Churchill, *Second World War*, Vol II, p4

CHAPTER NINE

Operation Seduction USA

1   Robert Sherwood, *Roosevelt and Hopkins*, p241

2   Thomas Parrish, *To Keep the British Isles Afloat*, p192

3   Lynne Olson, *Citizens of London*, p33

4   Gil Winant, *A Letter from Grosvenor Square*, p46

5   CSCT 3/43, 2 August (no year)

6   Sarah Churchill, *Keep On Dancing*, p159

7   Author's interview with John Julius Norwich

8   CSCT, 4 June 1944, letter from Mackenzie King to Clementine

9   Evelyn Waugh, letter to Nancy Mitford (date unknown), December 1950, Letters, p342

10 Averill Harriman, *Special Envoy*, p112

11 Doris Kearns Goodwin, *No Ordinary Time*, p11

12 Joseph Lash, *Eleanor and Franklin*, p664

CHAPTER TEN

From FDR to Stalin

1   Jon Meacham, *Franklin and Winston*, p228

2   Meacham, *Franklin and Winston*, pp236–7, interview with Mary Soames

3   Moran, *Struggle for Survival*, p151

4   Soames, *Clementine Churchill*, p379

5   Wheeler-Bennett (ed.), *Action This Day*, p157

6   Soames, *Clementine Churchill*, p385

7   Ibid., p386

8   Robert Bruce Lockhart, director of the Political Warfare Executive (in charge of propaganda), quoted in Alanbrooke, *War Diaries*, p474

9   Ibid., pix

10 Henry Morgenthau, *Mostly Morgenthaus*, p361

11 Morgenthau, *Diaries: Years of War*, p336

12 CSCT, 17 August 1944

13 Warren F. Kimball (ed.), *Churchill and Roosevelt: The Complete Correspondence*, Vol III, p332

14 Colville, *Fringes of Power*, p554

15 Ibid., p. 555

16 CSCT, 1 February 1945

17 Soames, *Clementine Churchill*, p404

18 CSCT, 2 April 1945

19 CSCT 3/37

20 CSCT, 8 May 1945

CHAPTER ELEVEN

A Private Line

1   Gerald Pawle, *The War and Colonel Warden*, p399

2   CSCT 3/56, 27 July 1945

3   Soames, *Clementine Churchill*, p428

4   Ibid., p429

5   Soames, *Clementine Churchill*, p443

6   CSCT, 12 September 1948

7   *W* magazine, 9–16 November 1979

8   Cecil Beaton, *Diaries 1948–55: The Strenuous Years*

9   Moran, *Struggle for Survival*, p494

10 Alastair Horne, *Macmillan 1894–1956*, Macmillan, 1988

11 Cecil Beaton, *Beaton in the Sixties*, p226

12 Moran, *Struggle for Survival*, xii

13 Martin Gilbert, *In Search of Churchill*, p316

14 Soames, *Clementine Churchill*, p528

15 Churchill, *Keep On Dancing*, p206

16 Beaton, *Beaton in the Sixties*, p17

17 Author's interview with Edwina Sandys

SELECT BIBLIOGRAPHY

Alanbrooke, Viscount,
War Diaries 1939–45, Weidenfeld & Nicolson, 2002

Asquith, H.H.,
Letters to Venetia Stanley, eds M. Brock and E. Brock,
Oxford University Press, 1988

Beaton, Cecil and Hugo Vickers,
*Beaton in the Sixties: The Cecil Beaton Diaries as He Wrote
Them, 1965–1969,* Weidenfeld & Nicolson, 2003

Bedell Smith, Sally,
Reflected Glory: The Life of Pamela Harriman,
Simon & Schuster, 1997

Best, Geoffrey,
Churchill: A Study in Greatness,
Oxford University Press, 2003

Churchill, Sarah,
Keep On Dancing, Weidenfeld & Nicolson, 1981

Churchill, Winston,
My Early Life, The Reprint Society, 1944

Churchill, Winston,
The Second World War Volume II: Their Finest Hour, Cassell, 1949

Colville, John,
*The Fringes of Power: 10 Downing Street Diaries
1939–1955,* W.W. Norton & Company, 1986

Cooper, Duff,
Diaries 1915–51, ed. John Julius Norwich,
Weidenfeld & Nicolson, 2006

Cooper, Lady Diana,
Trumpets from the Steep, Hart-Davis, 1960

Fishman, Jack,
My Darling Clementine, W.H. Allen, 1974

Gilbert, Martin,
In Search of Churchill, John Wiley, 1995

Gilbert, Martin,
Winston S. Churchill, Volume III, *The Challenge of War
1914–1916,* Heinemann, 1971

Gilbert, Martin,
Winston S. Churchill, Volume IV, *World in Torment
1916–1922,* Heinemann, 1975

Goodwin, Doris Kearns,
*No Ordinary Time, Franklin & Eleanor Roosevelt: The Home
Front in World War II,* Touchstone, Simon & Schuster, 1995

Harriman, William Averell and Elie Abel,
Special Envoy to Churchill and Stalin, 1941–1946,
Random House, 1972

Jackson, Ashley,
Churchill, Quercus, 2012

Kimball, Warren F. (ed.),
Churchill and Roosevelt: The Complete Correspondence, Volume
III, *Alliance Declining,* Princeton University Press, 1984

Lash, Joseph,
Eleanor and Franklin, Deutsch, 1972

Lee, Arthur Hamilton,
*'A Good Innings': The Private Papers of Viscount Lee of
Fareham,* ed. Alan Clark, John Murray, 1974

Meacham, Jon,
*Franklin and Winston: An Intimate Portrait
of an Epic Friendship,* Random House, 2004

Moran, Lord Charles,
Winston Churchill: The Struggle for Survival 1940–1965,
Simon & Schuster, 1982

Morgenthau, Henry,
Diaries: Years of War, 1941–1945, Houghton Mifflin, 1967

Morgenthau, Henry,
Mostly Morgenthaus: A Family History, Ticknor & Fields, 1991

Olson, Lynne,
*Citizens of London: The Americans Who Stood with Britain
in its Darkest, Finest Hour,* Random House, 2010

Olson, Lynne,
*Troublesome Young Men: The Rebels Who Brought
Churchill to Power and Helped Save England,*
Farrar Straus Giroux, 2007

Parrish, Thomas,
*To Keep the British Isles Afloat: FDR's Men
in Churchill's London. 1941,* Smithsonian, 2009

Pawle, Gerald,
The War and Colonel Warden, G.G. Harrap, 1963

Pearson, John,
Citadel of the Heart, Macmillan, 1991

Shelden, Michael,
Young Titan: The Making of Winston Churchill,
Simon & Schuster, 2013

Sherwood, Robert E.,
Roosevelt and Hopkins: An Intimate History,
Harper & Brothers, 1948

Soames, Mary,
Clementine Churchill, Doubleday, 2002

Soames, Mary (ed.),
*Speaking for Themselves: The Personal Letters of Winston
and Clementine Churchill*, Black Swan, 1999

Stelzer, Cita,
*Dinner with Churchill: Policy-Making at
the Dinner Table*, Short Books, 2011

Thompson, Walter H.,
Assignment: Churchill, Farrar, Straus & Young, 1955

Waugh, Evelyn,
The Letters of Evelyn Waugh, ed. Mark Amory,
Phoenix, 1980

Wheeler-Bennett, Sir John (ed.),
Action This Day: Working with Churchill,
Macmillan, 1968

Winant, John Gilbert,
A Letter from Grosvenor Square,
Houghton Mifflin, 1947

PICTURE CREDITS

8 Imagno/Getty Images 14 akg-images/Imagno 17 Keystone/Hulton Archive/Getty Images 19 Popperfoto/Getty Images 20 Fremantle/Alamy Stock Photo
23 National Trust/Charles Thomas 24 National Trust/Charles Thomas 25l National Trust/Charles Thomas 25r National Trust/Charles Thomas
27tl The Picture Art Collection/Alamy Stock Photo 27bl The Picture Art Collection/Alamy Stock Photo 27r Alto Vintage Images/Alamy Stock Photo
28 Illustrated London News Ltd/Mary Evans 31 Hulton-Deutsch Collection/Corbis/Getty Images 32 Illustrated London News Ltd/Mary Evans
33 Chronicle/Alamy Stock Photo 34 Fremantle/Alamy Stock Photo 36 Chronicle/Alamy Stock Photo 38 British Library, London/Diomedia 40 National
Portrait Gallery, London 43 Bettmann/Getty Images 44 W.G. Phillips/Topical Press Agency/Getty Images 45 Hulton Archive/Getty Images 46 Mirrorpix/
Bridgeman Images 47 Hulton Archive/Getty Images 48 Everett Collection Inc/Alamy Stock Photo 50 Interfoto/Alamy Stock Photo 53 Private Collection/
Roy Miles Fine Paintings/Bridgeman Images 55 Central Press/Getty Images 57 Ullstein Bild/Getty Images 58 PA Archive/PA Images 60 TopFoto
62 Hulton-Deutsch Collection/Corbis/Getty Images 65t TopFoto 65b TopFoto 66 PA Archive/PA Images 68 Illustrated London News Ltd/Mary Evans
72 Hulton Archive/Getty Images 74 Picture Post/Hulton Archive/Getty Images 75 PA Archive/PA Images 76-77 Nichols/Topical Press Agency/Getty Images
78 Fremantle/Alamy Stock Photo 79 G. Eric and Edith Matson Photograph Collection, Prints & Photographs Division, Library of Congress, LC-M32- 11693
81 PA Archive/PA Images 82-83 PA Archive/PA Images 84 PA Archive/PA Images 86-87 PA Archive/PA Images 88 Hulton Archive/Getty Images 91 Time Life
Pictures/The LIFE Images Collection/Getty Images 92 TopFoto 95 Andreas von Einsiedel/akg-images 96 Mirrorpix/Bridgexman Images 98 Bridgeman Images
99 Everett Collection Historical/Alamy Stock Photo 100 Central Press/Hulton Archive/Getty Images 101 Illustrated London News Ltd/Mary Evans 102 Hulton
Archive/Getty Images 103 Keystone-France/Gamma-Keystone/Getty Images 104 W.G. Phillips/Topical Press Agency/Getty Images 106-107 PA Archive/PA
Images 109 Mary Evans/SZ Photo/Scherl 110 Bettmann/Getty Images 112 PA Photos/TopFoto 113 Illustrated London News Ltd/Mary Evans 114 Yevonde
Portrait Archive/ILN/Mary Evans Picture Library 117 TopFoto 119 Mary Evans/SZ Photo/Scherl 120 Sport and General/S&G Barratts/EMPICS Archive/
PA Images 121 Keystone/Hulton Archive/Getty Images 122 IWM (P 554) 126-127 Hulton Archive/Getty Images 128 Popperfoto/Getty Images 131 Central
Press/Hulton Archive/Getty Images 132 Hulton-Deutsch Collection/Corbis/Getty Images 135 Popperfoto/Getty Images 136 Capt. Horton/IWM/Getty Images
138-139 Capt. Horton/IWM/Getty Images 140-141 Topical Press Agency/Getty Images 143 Keystone-France/Gamma-Rapho/Getty Images 144-145 Cecil
Beaton Studio Archive, Sotheby's London 146 Popperfoto/Getty Images 148 J.A. Hampton/Topical Press Agency/Getty Images 151 Fox Photos/Hulton
Archive/Getty Images 153 Anthony Wallace/Daily Mail/REX/Shutterstock 154 PastPix/TopFoto 157 Fox Photos/Getty Images 158 Everett Collection
Historical/Alamy Stock Photo 161 David E. Scherman/The LIFE Picture Collection/Getty Images 162-163 Hulton Archive/Getty Images 164 M. McNeill/
Fox Photos/Hulton Archive/Getty Images 166 Keystone/Hulton Archive/Getty Images 168 Popperfoto/Getty Images 171 PastPix/TopFoto 172 J. Wilds/
Keystone/Hulton Archive/Getty Images 173 Hulton-Deutsch Collection/Corbis/Getty Images 175 Major Horton/IWM/Getty Images 177 IWM (H 32954)
180 Bettmann/Getty Images 182 PA Photos/TopFoto 185 William Hustler and Georgina Hustler/National Portrait Gallery, London 186 Associated
Newspapers/REX/Shutterstock 189 Keystone/Hulton Archive/Getty Images 190 PA Archive/PA Images 193 Abbie Rowe/PhotoQuest/Getty Images
194 PA Archive/PA Images 195 William Sumits/The LIFE Picture Collection/Getty Images 196 Popperfoto/Getty Images 197 Central Press/Hulton Archive/
Getty Images 198 Popperfoto/Getty Images 199 Central Press/Hulton Archive/Getty Images 200 PNA Rota/Getty Images 203 Alfred Eisenstaedt/The LIFE
Picture Collection/Getty Images 204 Hulton Archive/Getty Images 206-207 Keystone-France/Gamma-Rapho/Getty Images 207 Keystone-France/Gamma-
Keystone/Getty Images 208 Popperfoto/Getty Images 210 Fox Photos/Getty Images 211 Ullstein Bild/Getty Images 213 George Rinhart/Corbis/Getty Images
214 TopFoto, 216 Reg Speller/Fox Photos/Hulton Archive/Getty Images 218-219 akg-images 221 Roger-Viollet/REX/Shutterstock 222-223 Romano Cagnoni/
Getty Images 223 Angelo Cozzi Giorgio Lotti Sergio Del Grande/Mondadori Portfolio/ Getty Images 224 Keystone-France/Gamma-Keystone/Getty Images
226-227 Keystone-France/Gamma-Keystone/Getty Images 228 National Portrait Gallery, London.

INDEX